# THE BEST GUIDE FOR
# MAKING MONEY IN THE 90's!

*A step by step guide to making huge profits retailing, wholesaling and exporting cars and trucks.*

by Timothy Johnson

**Published by:**

*Spirit Dance Publishing*
*P.O. Box 25036*
*Jackson, WY 83001*

Copyright © 1991 by Timothy Johnson

Printed in the United States of America

Library of Congress Catalog Card Number: 91-77164

ISBN 1-880782-07-3:    $17.95 softcover

# ACKNOWLEDGEMENTS

*I sincerely appreciate the cooperation, assistance and support of the governments of Canada, the U.S., Germany, Kuwait, Switzerland, the United Kingdom and Spain. I would also like to thank, Georgia Johnson, Ted Johnson and Travis and Bessie Yarbrough.*

Cover design and layout by:

Joy M. Johnson
P.O. Box 25036
Jackson Hole, Wy 83001.

# DISCLAIMER

This book was published to inform, educate and motivate. Every effort has been made to assure the accuracy of the material and facts contained herein, although it can not be guaranteed.

This book is not intended as a substitute for legal or other professional assistance. Anyone with legal, accounting or other professional questions, should seek competent professional advice.

## TO JOY

**WHOSE HELP WITH THIS EFFORT HAS BEEN IMMEASURABLE.**

# CONTENTS

# INTRODUCTION

You have chosen one of the most lucrative investment ideas for the nineties. For decades, only auto dealers and a few elite wholesalers have known about this incredible cash flow and profit making investment.

Before the 1970's, most people looked at real estate much the same way as people view automobiles today; it was a necessity we used for a purpose, not for an investment. Not many people back then understood the tremendous profits to be made investing in real estate, just as most people today don't understand the tremendous profits that can be made investing in automobiles.

The shrewd investors of the 70's and 80's, instead of just buying a house and making mortgage payments, invested in real estate and made outstanding financial gains. So too, will the smart investors of the 90's examine this new investment idea and, again, cash in on the tremendous profits. One big difference does exist: automobiles are very liquid, turnover is very quick and the paper work is uncomplicated.

The intent of this book is to teach you sound strategies for investing in cars and trucks with minimal exposure of cash outlay and maximum return of profits. The techniques in this book, if applied properly, will allow you to begin in your spare time and then if you so desire, evolve into a full time career.

There are three primary areas of investing in automobiles: retailing, wholesaling, and exporting. Just as I have, some of you may choose to invest in all three areas. For ease in understanding and application, we have discussed these three areas separately. Some areas of each may overlap and some techniques will apply to all three areas.

Study all three and then choose one of the areas that seems the most interesting to you. Concentrate and gain expertise in that area before moving on to the next. In this way, you'll avoid mistakes and disappointments and learn each area with a better understanding and confidence.

My sincere wish is that you will succeed and prosper using these techniques, just as I have.

# RETAILING

## INCLUDES

INVESTING FOR RETAIL, STEP BY STEP
WHAT SELLS IN YOUR AREA
WHERE TO LOOK
WHAT TO LOOK FOR
APPRAISING
PRICE GUIDES
NEGOTIATING PRICES
RECONDITIONING
ADVERTISE, ADVERTISE, ADVERTISE!
FUNDAMENTALS OF GOOD
SALESMANSHIP
COMPLETE THE PAPERWORK

# "THIS TIME, LIKE ALL TIMES, IS A VERY GOOD ONE, IF WE BUT KNOW WHAT TO DO WITH IT."

Ralph Waldo Emerson

# *INVESTING*

# *FOR*

# *RETAIL*

---

## *STEP BY STEP*

Money, money money! It never ever fails to amaze this writer how much money can be made everyday just by exchanging one vehicle for another. Equally amazing is the simplicity. No long drawn out transactions involving lawyers, accountants and other complicated factors.

Nearly 200 million vehicles are registered in the United States alone! Two or three vehicles in one family is not uncommon.

When most people decide to buy a car, they look in the paper or visit car dealerships in their area. They ask a few questions, then go for a test drive. Once a car is decided on, the buyer tries to negotiate a better price but usually ends up paying well above average retail. Next, the buyer allows the dealer or the banker to dictate the financing. Without questioning the interest rate or other terms of the loan, the buyer signs on the dotted line. The customer drives off happy to have the car they wanted. The only problem is, they paid too much for the car and then compounded the mistake by accepting financing that inflates their monthly payments and the total cost of the car. Sometime in the future, usually when they try to sell, they discover they've been had!

By following the simple guidelines presented here, you will never again pay too much for a car or truck. If you so choose, you'll never have another car payment in your life and you can still drive any car you want. More amazingly, you can even make money when you sell. Additionally, you can actually help the people who buy from you. They, in most cases, will pay below average retail and you can either help them arrange financing or advise them to shop interest rates and save even more money. This creates trust on their part and they will recommend you to their friends and relatives.

So, what is going on here? It really is quite simple. You will learn to shrewdly **buy vehicles at or below wholesale**. You can then **sell them at or below retail** and make a nice profit for yourself. The buyer who buys from you will usually pay less for the vehicle and save money on financing. As you can see, this is a winning transaction for everyone!

Retailing is a vast market encompassing many facets of the car investing business. New cars, used cars, fleet sales, rental cars, " buy here - pay here," financing, exotic and antique cars are to name just a few. As you discover and understand this business, some areas may be of more interest to you than others. This book will acquaint you with the major areas and teach you proven methods of success. You can then decide what is best suited for your particular interests.

The easiest and most comfortable market for most new investors is retailing. The purchases are easier because you can take your time and examine the vehicle thoroughly. You can then ascertain what it's worth and for how much it will sell. You can purchase and sell one unit at a time or have several to choose from, thereby, multiplying your profits much faster.

## NO CASH RETAILING

If you have money to get started, all the better. If not, some of the following methods will help or at least inspire you to think of some of your own. Having no money is only a problem if you perceive it that way. We have been taught that if we don't have money, we certainly can't invest in anything. Wrong! The real difference between having and not having money comes down to our determination and imagination in changing the problem. *Nothing is more thrilling than making something where most people believe nothing exists!* Keep your determination and motivation. If it has been taken away from you, reclaim it right now! Once it starts to happen for you, you'll never look back!

## SELL SOMETHING

That's right. Sell something you already own. Your mission here is to get some money to invest. It doesn't have to be a lot of money. Even several hundred dollars could be enough to get you started. Once you've made the system work for you, then you can replace whatever you had to sell.

## BORROW

If you have credit, obtain a business loan from your bank or finance company. Explain that you will use the money for business and investment purposes. Negotiate the interest rate and obtain the longest term possible. Most banks will require collateral for the loan. If they accept car titles as collateral, explain that you would like a line of credit with the bank releasing the titles once the credit line is paid down, by an agreed upon amount. Many banks will customize a loan to suit your particular needs. Talk to your banker, explain what you would like to do, then see what you can work out.

## CREDIT CARDS

Another good temporary source of quick cash is a

cash advance on your credit card. The interest rate will probably be high but you'll pay the money back quickly with the huge profits you are going to make. For example, say you obtain a cash advance of $800.00 on your Visa card. You then invest it in an inexpensive economy car. You sell it two weeks later for $1,200.00; giving you a gross profit of $400.00. The interest on the cash advance for two weeks will probably cost you less than $15.00, which is peanuts compared to the profit you just made. Is it worth it to put your credit to work? You bet it is!

## PARTNERS

One other possibility, is make temporary partners of friends, relatives and other investors. Tell them exactly what you intend to do and about how long you will need the money. To help them feel secure and excited about the possibilities, agree to let them keep the car title and in addition you'll give them a percentage of the profit! They're protected with collateral plus they get a tremendous return on their investment. I personally used this method when I got started. It worked so well that I had more investors than I could use! After acquiring adequate working capital through saving my profits, I discontinued using investor's money in favor of keeping more of the profits for myself.

## SELL DIRECTLY TO DEALERS.

Okay, if you don't have cash and you can't borrow any, try this technique. It involves locating a car or truck in your local newspaper, auto magazine or along the road. Talk to the owner and determine his rock bottom, immediate cash price. Using the techniques you will learn in this book, you'll know immediately the wholesale value of this particular car.

If the owner is willing to sell in the average or below average wholesale range, quickly call some dealers in the phone book or some that you may know about. Ask for the used car manager and ask him if he is interested in this particular car. Your call may go something like this: " Mr. Manager, my name is _____. I have a 1989 Ford Mustang convertible with 23,000 miles on it. Would this car be of interest to you?" Some will be interested, some will not. If yes, describe the car accurately and in detail. Try to get a price over the phone but if not, tell him you'll bring the car to him for his inspection and approval.

You should now tell the owner you would like to

drive the car and have it inspected. Also tell him you have someone else who is interested in the car or that you are an agent for a prospective buyer. Explain that you will tell this buyer about the car and show it to him, provided he will let you keep anything above the price you have already agreed on. If the owner gets what he wants, sells the car immediately and gets paid immediately, he probably won't care what you make. He wins and you win too!

With this agreement, you can now take the car to the dealer to get his opinion. So that you can maintain better control of the negotiations with the dealer, avoid if possible, bringing the owner with you. If the owner insists on coming anyway, ask him to wait in the dealer's office while you show the vehicle. Let the dealer tell you what he'll pay, then negotiate. Be honest with all concerned about this transaction. Tell the dealer you are an agent for the owner and you can't sell the car unless you make a profit for yourself. Frankly, the dealer doesn't care if you make money as long as he gets the car at a fair price so he can make a profit when he sells.

After agreeing on the price, which includes your profit, tell the dealer you will get the title and the owner and come back to complete the deal. Ask the dealer to issue two checks if possible; one for the amount due the owner and one to you for the difference. Next, bring the owner, the car and the title to the dealership to close the deal. That's all there is to it!

Congratulations! You have probably made a substantial profit using no cash and made a valuable contact (the dealer) for future business. This technique can also be used very effectively for wholesaling, which we will discuss in later chapters.

## CONSIGNMENT AGREEMENT

Another "no cash" technique that works well is the consignment agreement. Many f.s.b.o.'s (for sale by owner), don't know how to sell their car or truck or simply don't have the time or availability. You could literally open a car lot just selling consignments for individual owners!

To find people interested in consigning their vehicle, place an ad in the classifieds or call people with ads in classifieds and auto magazines. When you place your ad, make sure it states that you can sell their car or truck for them at no cost to them. Your ad should read something like this: " Wanted-Cars and Trucks! I can sell your car, easily and quickly. No Charge To You! Call 555-1212." Or you can try something like this: " Tired of trying to sell your car or truck? I can do it for you, Absolutely Free! Call 555-1212."

When an owner calls, explain what you do, which is act as an agent for sellers of cars and trucks. Explain to your callers that you help sellers connect with buyers who are ready and willing to buy immediately. Inform them that you maintain a list of buyers and often can create an instant sale. (You will be developing a valuable list of buyers, as you will see in a later section.)

Establish the owners rock bottom selling price with the condition you will call on any offers below that for their rejection or approval. You will need to look over and drive the vehicle to make sure it's worth what they want and still allow room for your profit. Suggest to them that they allow you to park the car where it will have good exposure and that your phone number will be displayed on the vehicle. Potential buyers can then call and get immediate information. As an incentive for them to give you the consignment, tell them you will advertise at absolutely no charge to them. Additionally, your phone is answered twenty-four hours a day! Moreover, you will call them each time you show the car and keep them informed of any comments which might help sell the vehicle.

A brief and simple consignment agreement should be presented and signed by the owner and you. Consignment forms can be found at most office supply stores or you can make up your own. You can also modify the standard consignment forms to meet your requirements.

I have used consignment agreements in the past with excellent cash profits. In fact, you could earn a nice living just by working consignments. I had my first consignment when I was only seventeen years old and working at a local gas station. I sold a customer's Corvette and received a $100.00 commission, which in the sixties wasn't too bad!

As with all techniques in this book, you must implement the basics of good marketing, i.e.: freshly detailed vehicles, positive attitude, politeness and good salesmanship, all of which are explained in later chapters. If you use these ingredients, you'll easily make big profits using these "no cash" techniques for retailing. Note: there are other "no cash" techniques that will be discussed in later chapters on wholesaling.

All the methods and information discussed so far apply equally to starting without cash and having money to work with. Learn these fundamental steps thoroughly and you will be on your way to financial success in retailing, wholesaling and exporting!

# WHAT SELLS IN YOUR AREA

---

Build a better mouse trap and the world will beat a path to your door. In retailing, providing what is in demand is a very important ingredient to your success. A great purchase on your part is only great if it's something that sells well in your area. Buying a cute little red convertible below wholesale in Florida, for example, would assure a quick and substantial profit. Doing the same thing in Anchorage, Alaska, might not be nearly so successful. My point is this: **buy what sells good in your area.** Consider this; if you live in snow country or mountainous areas; how about four-wheel drives? For sunny or warm climates; how about sports cars and convertibles? Blue-collar areas; try economical money savers and pick-ups. Up-scale areas; maybe you should try luxury cars and specialty vans. Retirement communities; how about four door sedans with safety and comfort options. While most vehicles can be sold anywhere, some will sell better than others. In the beginning, so that you can increase your chances of success, you should concentrate on the most popular vehicles in your area.

Many other factors affect what might sell in your area. Begin finding out by talking to car dealers (used car managers). Ask what kinds of cars and trucks they would like to buy and what people are asking for when they come in. Attend auto auctions and read the local classified to get an understanding of what is being bought and sold. Look around and begin noticing what people are driving. Lastly, as you begin to buy and sell, your customers will let you know what they're looking for. **Note:** An exception to this rule would be an area where a segment of the market is being overlooked. Suppose you live in a town where dealers have already covered the most popular vehicle market. Although you can still do quite well in this market, you could consider specializing in what no one else is handling. For example, the sports car market in Anchorage, Alaska may be small but if no one else is covering this segment, you could consider testing it to see if it is worthwhile.

A dealer I know in Florida does a tremendous business reconditioning and selling nothing but older Volkswagens. Still another, will only buy and sell British made sports cars.

*BETTER TO BE UNBORN
THAN UNTAUGHT FOR
IGNORANCE IS THE ROOT OF
MISFORTUNE*

*PLATO*

# WHERE
# TO
# LOOK

---

In retailing, there is an abundance of sources for your purchases. We'll cover most of them here and you will discover additional sources as you gain experience.

As you study this book you will see that many of these sources can be used with or without cash. These sources can also be used later for wholesale selling; especially the following three: new car trades, auctions and wholesalers. I have used all the sources listed here and I prefer some over the others. I suggest that you try all of them and find out which ones seem to work best for you.

Again, I think it's best to start simply and work your way up.

I'll never forget one of my first money-makers. I was a full-time college student living in a rented apartment with two roommates. I had just been fired from my part-time job as a shoe salesman and, needless to say, feeling a bit depressed. On my way home, I saw parked on a side street, a '71 Mercury Capri with a for sale sign in the window. I stopped and casually looked the car over. It was filthy inside and out and had a broken side glass. The owner came out and we began to talk. It had been his son's car and his son no longer lived in the states. They just wanted to get rid of it. The owner realized the car didn't look good and stated he would take $900.00. I explained that I didn't have $900.00 and that the car needed work, however, I would be willing to pay $550.00. I pointed out to him that he could actually save money by selling it now because he could cancel the insurance and not have to renew the tag; plus the car deteriorated a little more every day. He went inside to discuss it with his wife and returned shortly with a counter-offer of $600.00. I accepted his counter-offer and went home to gather every penny I had, which was only about $400.00. I borrowed $250.00 from my roommate and returned to pick up my new *investment*. I drove the car home, cleaned it thoroughly inside and out, replaced the broken glass, put an ad in the newspaper and sold it for $1,200.00 - all within one week! I made a net profit of $563.00! (A selling price of $1,200.00 less cost of $600.00, less repairs of $37.00) I repaid the loan from my roommate and now had $1,000 to reinvest. Needless to say, I felt great! I followed up by buying two more inexpensive cars and doing the same thing all over again. I was on my way! The same opportunities exist in every city across the country!

The following sources are random and importance should not be placed on the order in which they are listed. Depending on where you are located, some of these sources will be more beneficial than others.

## AUTOMOBILE MAGAZINES AND CLASSIFIED ADS

Scan the ads  and circle as many cars and trucks as possible that are interesting to you. With these possibilities you can now begin to call the owners with a checklist of questions. Refer to the checklist I have included on the next page. Call the owners and get answers to these questions without wasting valuable time looking at cars that are not possibilities.

## Checklist Questions

** What is the year-make-model-color?

** What is the current mileage?

** Does the vehicle have body damage?

** Has the vehicle had previous body damage?

** How do you rate the vehicle mechanically?

** What size engine?

** Type of transmission: automatic or manual?

** Condition of the interior?

** Condition of the tires?

** What kind of options and equipement?

** Do you have service records?

** Asking Price?

** Are you willing to negotiate?

Based on the answers to these questions, you can now decide whether it is feasible to examine this vehicle further.

## RUN YOUR OWN ADVERTISEMENT

Placing an ad is a good technique for finding car owners who are needing to sell immediately and therefore, for a discounted price. Your ad might say something like: "Wanted! I will buy your car or truck immediately! Call 555-1234."
When someone calls, ask them the checklist questions on page 34. If the vehicle seems to be a possibility, make an appointment to inspect it. When you arrive for the inspection; introduce yourself, look the car over and drive it. Using the inspection techniques on page 52 and the appraisal procedures discussed on page 59, determine the value and purchase the car within these guidelines. If you do not have enough money to buy the car and cannot get it, use one of the "no cash" techniques discussed previously.

## **BANKS AND FINANCE COMPANY REPOSSESSIONS**

Unfortunately, thousands of cars and trucks are repossessed everyday. Since these vehicles are depreciating assets, the banks and finance companies must liquidate these vehicles as quickly as possible. The bank's loss can become your gain if you know what to do!

You should first call the banks in your area. Start with your bank and ask if they have any repossessed cars or trucks. Ask to speak to the person who handles the selling and bidding of these vehicles. Talk with this person and find out where the vehicles are located, the purchasing procedure and any other information that could be helpful. Next, you should look the vehicles over. Some banks have areas the size of football fields - full of cars! Don't bother asking specific questions about the condition of any of the cars, the bankers probably don't know. Once you have decided which vehicles interest you, determine repair cost, if any. Refer to page 55, for an example of determining repair costs. Next, determine wholesale and retail value using one or both of the wholesale guides on page 64.

Some banks will simply tell you an asking price for each vehicle, while others will require you to submit a bid of how much you are willing to pay. If the bank tells you an asking price, you can compare it to your wholesale value, which you have already determined. Next, try to negotiate the banks asking price to get at or below your wholesale value. For example, you have looked over a 1988 Suzuki 4x4. The bank has an asking price of $3,500.00 and you have determined the wholesale value to be $3,200.00.

Even though you know you can sell the vehicle quickly for $3,900.00, you should still negotiate and try to get the vehicle for its wholesale value.

If it is a bid process, simply complete the bid sheet indicating the most you are willing to pay. Keep in mind, more bids will be submitted and the bank will take the highest bid as of a certain date. Consider bidding unusual amounts in order to top bids close to yours. For example, instead of $3000.00, submit a bid of $3011.00. This way, if another wholesaler has submitted a bid of $3,000.00 (rounded numbers are the most common) your bid would be the one accepted because it is higher.

Once your offer is accepted, you must pay for the vehicle as soon as possible; usually within twenty-four hours. Banks sometime accept sight drafts but generally want to be paid with a cashiers check or cash. If you are short on cash, you can try "no cash" technique #3 on page 21. Occasionally, you can make an agreement with a bank or finance company to act as an agent in dispensing of their repossessed vehicles. Talk to the person in charge and negotiate either a set fee or you retain any profit above a certain price.

You will discover that bank and finance company repossessions can be a great source for all types of vehicles for both retailing and wholesaling. You will be thrilled and amazed the first time you buy a repo and sell it the same day for a huge profit! I know it works. I've done it many, many times!

## WHOLESALERS-NEW CAR DEALERS-AUCTIONS

The tremendous profits and fast action of the sources we are about to discuss can apply to both retail and wholesale. We will cover areas here that may seem complex right now, but by the time you finish this guide, everything will be crystal clear and easily understood. Read this section now, then come back to it after reading the wholesale chapters.

## WHOLESALERS

Another very good source of a great variety of cars and trucks is licensed wholesalers. That sounds great but, what are licensed wholesaler and where do you find them?

Licensed wholesalers are actually licensed auto and truck dealers that specialize in wholesale transactions from dealer to dealer, dealer to auction, and auction to auction.

Wholesaling can be a small operation that is part-time, selling only a few vehicles weekly or monthly or it can be very large and sell hundreds of vehicles weekly or monthly. Wholesalers generally prefer to sell to dealers or at auctions because of the quick cash flow and the fast profits. Some, however, wholesale and retail. Wholesalers usually have a broad range of cars and trucks and their inventory changes very quickly.

To locate wholesalers in your area; look in the phone book under the heading of automobiles; then look for brokers, agents or wholesalers. You also can call the Department of Motor Vehicles in your state or county. Ask for the names, addresses, and telephone numbers of licensed wholesalers in your area.

One of the best ways to find wholesalers is to visit new car dealerships in your town. Wholesalers visit new car dealerships daily to buy and sell cars and trucks. Talk to the used car manager and ask him to recommend a few reputable wholesalers. If he asks why you want to know, just be honest. Explain to him that you are interested in working with a wholesaler or becoming one yourself. You could also mention that you would also like to purchase any vehicles he would like to wholesale. Since wholesalers are coming and going all day, the manager may introduce you to somebody while you are there.

After you have located a wholesaler, introduce yourself and explain that you are interested in buying cars and trucks for resale and later on you might be interested in wholesaling as well. Explain to him that you are relatively new at this, and for now you would like to buy one car at a time, retail it, then buy another and so on. Most will be receptive to your plan, because, for them, you will be another profitable outlet.

## NO CASH TECHNIQUE

At the same time you talk to him about buying cars, explain that you also would like to make a list of the cars and trucks he has available and what he would accept for each of these vehicles. Explain further, that you would like to show these vehicles to retail customers. In this way, you could sell these cars for him and be entitled to all the profits over his set price! If he does not want you to take the cars away for showing, you can bring your customers to where the cars are located.

If the wholesaler accepts your offer (he probably will), you'll now have an endless supply of fresh cars and trucks to show your retail customers and you have absolutely no cash invested! When you sell vehicles owned by other wholesalers, they handle all the paperwork. All you need to do is accept a check for your share of the profits!

**Note:** Since you now have a list of vehicles, make it work to your advantage. When customers call regarding cars you have advertised, but have been sold already, tell them about the cars on your list. No cash invested, extra sales and extra profits!

IMPORTANT: Your relationship with wholesalers can be very profitable both now and later when you begin wholesaling and exporting. At some point, as you gain experience and your sales volume increases, you will need to decide whether to obtain your dealer's license or reach an agreement to be an agent or broker for a particular wholesaler. For a more in depth explanation of licensing, see page 95.

### NEW CAR TRADES

This source of cars and trucks is one of the largest and is the favorite of most wholesalers throughout the U.S.. New car dealers receive trade-ins on just about every new car and truck they sell. The new car dealers wholesale these trade-ins for a variety of reasons; cash flow, wrong type of vehicle for their inventory, too old, etc.. The point is this: They sell these trade-ins promptly and usually below wholesale! Wholesalers visit new car dealerships daily to buy and place these vehicles to other dealers and auctions.

Once you become familiar with how the trade-in system works, you can make huge profits everyday, both wholesaling and retailing. Start by introducing yourself to the used car manager or the person in charge of wholesaling. Explain that you are interested in buying his trade-ins. Most of these dealers will only wholesale to licensed dealers or an agent of a licensed wholesaler. However, some new car dealers may allow you to purchase from them without the licensing requirements. The only way to really find out is to go to the dealerships in your area and talk to the used car manager. Frankly, the best way to have access to these big profit makers is to be licensed or become an agent for a wholesaler in your area. Everything you need to know about licensing is contained in the wholesale section of this book.

## DEALER AUCTIONS

If you have ever been to a large dealer auction, you will probably know what I mean when I say it's like trading on the New York Stock Exchange. Tremendous profits and huge quantities of vehicles are bought and sold in a matter of hours. Wholesalers, agents of wholesalers, retail dealers, banks and fleet liquidators all meet here to buy and sell from each other. Here is one example of the potential profits to be made at these auctions: I bought a 1988 Nissan Sentra at one auction and took it to a different auction for the following sale. I sold it there for a $1,600.00 profit!

Auctions can be a great source of cars and trucks, especially if you have a retail customer who is looking for a particular make, color or style. I have had buyers waiting with cash in hand for cars I have bought at auctions. Again, you will need to be a licensed dealer, wholesaler or the agent of a licensed dealer to buy and sell at dealer auctions.

Since dealer auctions are designed for and derive their income from licensed dealers, it is easy to understand why most auctions do not permit you to bring retail buyers on the property on sale day. Find out the rules of the auctions you attend and respect those rules. You'll soon discover they exist for your protection as well as the other dealers attending.

## DEALER AUCTIONS, STEP BY STEP

Assuming that you have never been to or participated in a dealer auction, the best way to become acquainted is to walk through the procedure step by step.

Locate the auctions in your area through other dealers, The Department of Motor Vehicles, or the phone book. See the Appendix for a partial listing of dealer auctions throughout the U.S. and Canada. Many cities also have a National Independent Automobile Dealers Association(NIADA) office. Most of these offices can help you locate dealer auctions in your area. You may want to be a member of NIADA if you become licensed. See the Appendix for further information on NIADA.

Call or go to the auctions for registration so that you can buy and sell. If you have just received your dealers license, some auctions will want to place you on a cash basis for a trial period or until they are able check your bank references. If you are an agent for a wholesaler, he will have to register you. Once registered, you will receive an auction card that identifies you and gives you buying and selling privileges.

Now for the buying and selling. Dealer auctions are very fast paced. Hundreds and sometimes many thousands of vehicles will pass through a single auction in one day. The best way to get your feet wet is to attend a few auctions and observe all the action around you. Don't bid on anything yet; this is just for fun and experience.

Vehicles sold at auctions are divided into lanes usually by year or type. Each car or truck in a particular lane then receives a number in the sequence in which it will cross the auction block. For example, lane "A" might be for cars 1988 or newer. So a car labeled A-110, will run in the "A" lane and will be the 110th car to cross the block.

Locate a car (or several for that matter) that has not yet crossed the auction block. Appraise it using the wholesale price guides you now have, taking into account any needed repairs as well as mileage, appearance and overall "eye appeal". Using this information, determine what you think the wholesale value should be and what you would be willing to pay for the car and still make a profit.

Next, write down the lane number and the run number and wait for the car to come across the block. You can even estimate how long it will take for a vehicle to come up. For instance, if each vehicle takes two minutes on the block, then it will take about two hundred twenty minutes (3 hours, 40 minutes) before vehicle A-110 will cross the block. Some auctions provide a convenient little printed card (bid sheet), which helps to keep track of the cars that are of interest to you. They are usually located in the auction office and are free for the asking.

Now that you have listed cars that interest you, follow them as they come to the block. **Caution**: note the light system for each auction and listen for special announcements about the vehicle when it arrives on the block. Be sure you know what the lights mean for each auction you attend. They are most often located above or next to the block.

Usually but not always, they look like and mean the following.

**Green:** Sold as a sound vehicle. Buyer may test drive and arbitrate if a problem exist.

**Yellow:** Caution; announced conditions exist, otherwise the vehicle is sound.

**Red:** Sold as is; no warranty of any kind. Possible mechanical, frame or body damage. No arbitration.

**Blue:** Title is not present.

**White:** Indicates mileage in excess of 100,000 miles or the true mileage is unknown.

One of the cars you are interested in has arrived on the block. The light system is set, announcements are made and other buyers are looking and getting ready to bid. Listen intently as the bidding begins. Each car stays on the block about two minutes or less. If the auctioneer announces "sold"; jot down the selling price next to your "practice bid". Is it close to the selling price? High? Low? Analyze and continue to practice until you feel comfortable bidding on cars you would really like to buy. **Note:** As you become more confident, you will learn the subtle intricacies of dealer auctions. You will develop your own bidding strategies that work best for you.

If you are the high bidder, then you sign in at the auction block and receive a buyer's copy of the sale. The buyer's copy will contain a description of the car, how much you paid and the conditions of the sale. If the purchase was with a drive (green light), then drive the car to make sure it is mechanically sound. Be sure to check it thoroughly for frame damage or any other item allowed under the auction rules. If the car checks out properly, proceed to the auction office to pay for the vehicle. You can usually pay for your purchases by draft, check or cash.

If the car appears to have a problem, take it **immediately to the arbitration office.** Arbitration will drive the car and using an independent mechanic, determine if the problem exists or not. If a problem does exist and you purchased the vehicle on a green light, you may ask for a price adjustment that you deem reasonable or you can decline to purchase the car. If arbitration does not find anything wrong with the car, then you must purchase the car at your original bid price. **Note:** Light systems and arbitration rules vary slightly from auction to auction. Read the rules of each auction before you bid.

For some, dealer auctions may seem difficult to manage. On the other hand, with time and practice, auctions can become one of the quickest and most profitable places to buy and sell. I could give you countless examples of profits of $1,000.00 or more on cars that I have bought at auctions. With practice, you will soon have your own stories to tell!

## GOVERNMENT AUCTIONS

I have attended many government auctions and have never been too impressed. The auction nets about 80% of the retail value, on a consistent basis. Needless to say, that will not leave a lot of room for big profits. You can spend your time much better buying from other sources. Occasionally, however, you can obtain a good buy from a government auction. As with dealer auctions, you should arrive early to inspect and appraise the vehicles of interest to you. Government auction rules are similar to dealer auction rules, but be sure to pick up a copy of the rules and procedures when you sign in.

Some government agencies maintain a mailing list and will notify you of pending auctions. Get on the mailing list of those who maintain them by calling or writing that government agency. Other government agencies do not maintain a mailing list but instead, advertise in local and national newspapers such as U.S.A. Today, The Wall Street Journal and, sometimes, car magazines.

One source of government auctions worth looking into is your local county and city government. In some communities, especially smaller ones, participating bidders are minimal. Consequently, the prices can be very low.

Contact the different government departments in your town such as the sheriffs department, fire department, etc. and find out how to purchase confiscated and excess vehicles.

The sources we have discussed here are some of the most important you will encounter. There are many more, such as rental fleet sales, state and city auctions, utility and telephone company sales, theft/recovery auctions and more. They are fairly easy to find by simply contacting insurance companies, local and state government agencies, etc.. You only need to ask them where they sell the vehicles they no longer wish to own.

**NOTE:** If you are completely new to investing in automobiles, I recommend you begin with the basics and keep your purchases and sales transactions simple. Use some of the simplest strategies first, then as you gain experience and confidence, move on to the more complicated transactions.

# *WHAT*
# *TO*
# *LOOK*
# *FOR*

## CHOOSE WINNERS - AVOID LEMONS

Two crucial elements of your money-making strategy, is to avoid lemons and avoid spending too much time and money reconditioning your vehicles. You will develop your own procedure as you gain experience, but for now, I would recommend the following basic steps.

1. Don't look at any vehicle on a rainy day or at night, when lighting is especially poor. You can't see body damage or spot other problems such as oil leaks or bad tires.

2. Do not start the vehicle as soon as you arrive. Walk all the way around the car looking for dents, rust or previous body work.

3. Look for broken or cracked glass.

4. Look at the interior for wear, stains or cuts.

5. Open the trunk. Check for a spare tire and jack.

6. Inspect the tires for a matching set and wear.

7. Look under the car for oil leaks and frame damage.

8. Open the hood. Look for oil leaks, rust and body damage.

9. Check the oil. Is it full? Dirty? Milky in appearance? If it has a strange appearance, milky for example, the car could have a serious engine problem. Unless you deduct from the value for a major repair or have the ability to repair it yourself, you should delete this car from your list. (Older cars may have some oil

underneath, but don't buy cars with puddles unless, again, you have deducted enough for a major repair.)

10. Check the radiator. Is it rusty; Full? Radiators should be full of coolant or water. Anything else indicates a problem. Deduct for the repair or delete the vehicle from your list.

11. Check the transmission fluid. Is the fluid clear? Full? Does it smell burned?

12. Finally, start the car. Turn the radio off before starting so you can listen intently for any unusual noises from the engine, transmission and clutch. Note anything unusual for further inspection while test driving.

13. Check the transmission. With your foot on the brake, put the vehicle in reverse. It should engage immediately, with firmness. Now, put it in drive. It should engage the same way. If anything seems abnormal, yet the vehicle seems good overall, take the car to a transmission shop while you test drive it. If you tell the shop you're a dealer, you can receive a dealer's discount.

14. Check the clutch. Listen for noises.

15. Test the horn, lights and all electronics for correct operation.

16. While test driving the vehicle, note anything unusual about the brakes, steering, clutch or rear end noise. If you cannot diagnose the problem, again, take it to a mechanic for his opinion.

17. Check the speedometer, odometer, fuel gauge, air conditioning, heater, and other any other options the car may have, i.e., power windows, sunroof, etc..

The more vehicles you inspect, the better you will become at spotting problems and estimating costs of repairs. Until then, don't hesitate to get estimates and seek opinions from other people who can help. Refer to the checklist on the following page to help you develop good inspection habits.

## CONDITION CHECKLIST

<u>YEAR</u>   <u>MAKE</u>   <u>MODEL</u>   <u>MILES</u>   <u>PRICE</u>

| CONDITION | CLEAN | AVG | POOR | REPAIR EST. $ |
|-----------|-------|-----|------|----------------|
| BODY | | | | |
| PAINT | | | | |
| GLASS | | | | |
| INTERIOR | | | | |
| TIRES | | | | |
| ENGINE | | | | |
| TRANS. | | | | |
| A/C | | | | |
| BRAKES | | | | |
| HEATER | | | | |
| OTHER | | | | |

TOTAL EST. REPAIRS $_____

OWNERS NAME: _____

ADDRESS & PH:_____

DIRECTIONS TO VEHICLE:

# IT IS HARD TO FAIL BUT IT IS WORSE NEVER TO HAVE TRIED TO SUCCEED.

*Theodore Roosevelt*

# *APPRAISING*

## WHAT'S IT WORTH?

Ask five wholesalers or retail dealers what a particular car is worth and you'll probably get five different answers. However, if they are seasoned pro's, their answers will be very close.

Car and truck appraising is an art with many variables that influence value. Take, for example, a 1988 Subaru Justy 4x4, being offered for sale in Florida. It's very clean, has low miles, but does not have air conditioning. Local Florida dealers will deduct heavily because it lacks air conditioning. However, if the same car was offered for sale in Michigan, or a northern dealer was appraising the car for resale in a cooler climate, the fact that the car is without air conditioning would not affect its value nearly as much. Hence, you would receive two considerably different appraisals of the same vehicle. Once you master the art of accurately appraising your vehicles, you'll be on your way to making huge profits time after time.

If I had to choose one area of car investing that is critical to success, I would have to choose appraising. With accurate appraising and shrewd price negotiating, you can virtually guarantee instant profits as fast as you can move the car from one location to another! In retailing, wholesaling and exporting, I have proved this over and over again. Allow me to give you an example of what good appraising can do for you. I have had countless occasions when I have sold to a dealer for various amounts of profits, (but often averaging about $500.00), **the very car I arrived in.** Since I am now without a vehicle, I will price cars and trucks he would like to wholesale and then call other dealers to see if they are interested. Finding an interested dealer, I drive it to his dealership and sell it for a profit of say, $300.00. I haven't even bought the car yet, but look at what has happened. I made a $500.00 profit on my car that I sold to the first dealer, I took a car he needed to sell and

sold it to a second dealer for another profit of $300.00.
Dealer number "2" gets a fresh car for his inventory, dealer
"1" gets rid of a car he no longer wants and I make a total
profit of $800.00 - Everybody Wins! You can literally do
this all day long, everyday of the week! The key element
here is knowing what a car or truck is worth, buying it for
less and then selling it quickly to a ready buyer.

Accurate appraising involves many factors, some of
which are; inspecting carefully the vehicles you purchase,
knowing what your clients want and understanding your
local car market.

## APPRAISING, STEP BY STEP

1. Use the wholesale guides referred to on page 63. Other
   guides are available but these are the most widely used.
2. Classify the vehicle, factoring in overall appearance and
   appeal.
3. Buy what sells in your area. Remember, just because
   you like a particular car, doesn't mean somebody else
   will.
4. Considering the above factors, deduct repair costs and
   get-ready costs.

5. Finally, ask yourself what you can quickly sell the vehicle for (retail or wholesale) after you get it ready.

Remember: The difference between what you are willing to pay (plus repair costs) and what you can **realistically** sell it for, will be your profit. Make sure this is a figure you will be satisfied with.

**IMPORTANT NOTE:** Be sure to deduct accurately for high mileage and add value for low mileage. Keep in mind that most new car dealers will not purchase high mileage vehicles.

As you become more experienced, your ability to make accurate appraisals will develop quickly. With many vehicles you will know instantly what it's worth and how much profit you can make.

To help you develop good appraisal skills for both retail and wholesale, use the guidelines on the following page for estimating wholesale value and estimating expected profit.

# WHOLESALE VALUE ESTIMATOR

## YEAR   MAKE   MODEL   MILES

WHOLESALE VALUE                    ____

LESS REPAIRS                       ____

LESS HIGH MILES                    ____

ADD LOW MILES                      ____

**WHOLESALE VALUE (AS IS)**        ____

---

# EXPECTED PROFIT  ESTIMATOR

READY RETAIL VALUE                 ____

LESS COST OF VEHICLE               ____

COST OF REPAIR                     ____

OTHER: ADVERT., ETC.               ____

**EXPECTED PROFIT**                ____

## "FAILURE IS NOT THE ONLY PUNISHMENT FOR LAZINESS: THERE IS ALSO THE SUCCESS OF OTHERS."

*Jules Renard, 1898*

# WHOLESALE
# &
# RETAIL
## PRICE GUIDES

---

## HOW TO GET THEM

To help appraise cars and trucks more accurately, dealers and wholesalers use pricing guides with a proven record of reliability. Some regions prefer one over the other. The two most widely used are the National Automobile Dealers Used Car Guide, commonly referred to as N.A.D.A., and the Black Book Guide.

63

## N.A.D.A.

Published monthly, the N.A.D.A Guide is used not only by dealers, but also by banks and credit unions. N.A.D.A. determines the average loan value, the average trade-in value and the average retail value in different regions of the U.S.. These values are based on reports of actual transactions in each region.

N.A.D.A. Guide also has a suggested dollar deduction for high mileage and suggested dollar add-on for low mileage. The format is easy to read and understand. Be careful to classify your vehicle accurately so that you can determine accurate values.

A one year subscription, at this writing, costs $43.00.

To order: Call toll-free 1-800-544-6232

In Virginia: 1-800-523-3110

Or write: N.A.D.A.

       8400 Westpark Drive

       McLean, VA 22102-9985

N.A.D.A. will bill you or they accept M/C, Visa and American Express.

## THE BLACK BOOK

The Black Book Guide classifies vehicles into four different categories: Extra clean, clean, average and rough, and attaches a wholesale dollar value to each classification. Optional equipment is also given a dollar value and added to the base value. Conversely, lack of equipment is given a dollar value and deducted from the base value. The guide is indexed for quick, easy reference and lists, extensively, both domestic and foreign cars.

Black Book Car Guide also publishes a separate truck and van guide with an extensive listing of most every truck and van; import and domestic. The Black Book Guide is published weekly, while The Black Book Truck and Van Guide is published twice monthly. Both guides are regional and therefore reflect the prices of cars and trucks in your area of the country. If you desire, you may order black books for different regions, for example, the southeast region or the Pacific Northwest. The Black Book representative will be glad to help you and perhaps give you a sample copy of each region.

A one year subscription to Black Book costs $69.00. A one year subscription to Black Book Truck and Van costs

$55.00. To order, call 1-800-554-1026, except Georgia. In Georgia, call 1-404-532-4111. Or write: National Auto Research, P.O. Box 758, Gainesville, Georgia 30503.

I suggest that you subscribe to both guides, at least for now. This way you can cross reference using both guides for greater accuracy. You may also find one guide preferred over the other in your area. **Hint:** If you can't afford to subscribe to either guide right now, check with your local library. Most libraries have a monthly copy of the N.A.D.A. Guide. If you have met a wholesaler or used car manager, ask him if you can have his old copy when his new one arrives.

# *NEGOTIATING PRICES*

You've inspected the car, driven it, determined its wholesale and retail value and how much profit you can make. The only other obstacle is the owner, Mr. Smith, who is asking more then you want to pay. Now what? Negotiating involves compromises by both parties. One approach, which is very direct, honest and logical, is this: Explain to Mr. Smith that you will have to do certain repairs and based on that, is he willing to negotiate. If not, leave your name and phone number, thank him for his time and leave. Most owners, however, are willing to negotiate. Show or explain to Mr. Smith what you'll have to do and how much it will cost, approximately. Point out flaws the car might have, such as bad paint, cracked glass, bad tires, high mileage, etc.. Tell him that you can buy the car **right now!** Offer less than you are willing to pay. More than likely, he will reject it and "counter" with his own offer. Finally, you will agree or reach the highest price you can afford to pay and still make a profit. Again, if you can't agree, be polite and leave your name and number. Explain to him you have several more cars to look at, but your offer is good for 24 hours. Now you should leave. One important point: Do not get emotionally attached to any car that you are trying to purchase. You will pay more for the car than it is worth and gain little profit, if any. Always move on to the next one if you can't agree on the price.

With the exception of the "no cash" methods, you should either pay for your vehicles by personal check, cashiers check or sight draft. Avoid paying in cash whenever possible. If something goes wrong, proof of payment becomes much more difficult to verify. Pay for the vehicle only after you have inspected the title. Compare the v.i.n. number on the car, to the v.i.n number on the title. Make sure the signature is exactly correct and notarized, if necessary. Have the owner sign a Bill of Sale and an odometer statement. Make sure any liens on the title have been paid. These forms can usually be found at an office supply store or a dealer auction. You can also have them printed. See the Appendix for an illustration.

Sight drafts are usually used when you buy from a dealer or wholesaler. This banking instrument looks very much like an ordinary check, but serves various other functions. Please refer to the Appendix for an illustration and wholesaling on page 100 for a thorough explanation of sight drafts.

# THE WAY TO BE NOTHING IS TO DO NOTHING.

*Nathaniel Howe*

# *RECONDITIONING*

Life is great! You've made your first purchase. It's a great car and you know you are going to make a huge profit! Lets finish the job.

## GET READY

Get ready is the process of preparing the car or truck for resale. Everything from mechanical repairs, to detailing and advertising needs to be completed as quickly as possible. The faster you can get them ready, the faster you can sell, the faster your profits will accumulate!

Do mechanical repairs first, then cosmetics such as body and interior repair. Lastly, detail the car thoroughly. Shop for prices on all repairs and parts. Tell the shop you are a dealer and that you will give them plenty of repeat business if they will give you a discount. Whether this is a part-time or a full time business, you might consider getting a sales tax number. By becoming tax-exempt, you can save thousands of dollars on just about everything you purchase related to your cars. See Sales Tax Exempt on page 97.

To save money, consider detailing the vehicle yourself, if you have the time and ability. If not, there are plenty of detail shops available. Prices range from $25.00 to $150.00 depending on where you are located and how much the vehicle needs. A detailer will thoroughly clean the interior, exterior, trunk, engine and tires. They wax, shampoo carpets, deodorize, remove road grime and much more. When a detail shop is finished, your car should look as new as possible. **Hint:** There are many things you can do to enhance the appearance of your vehicle and therefore its' value. Consider accent stripes, upgraded wheel covers, and other accessories as long as they pay off. You'll be surprised how easy it is to turn a plain, boring car into a real eye-catcher.

## PRICING

Your car comes out of the detail shop looking like a dream car! It's been serviced mechanically and is ready to go. One last look and your are ready to set a definite asking price. You already determined a retail price when you were buying it. However, you may want to make an adjustment if you spent more money getting it ready or it turned out much better than you expected. Review the price guide books to make sure you are within the guideline price. Price accordingly, factoring in how fast you want to sell and the appeal and popularity of the vehicle.

**Hint:** For quick sales, look at advertisements for other vehicles like yours. Try to price yours for just a little less, but still leave room to negotiate and make a good profit.

# "NOTHING WILL EVER BE ATTEMPTED IF ALL POSSIBLE OBJECTIONS MUST BE FIRST OVERCOME"

Dr. Johnson, 1759

# ADVERTISE!
# ADVERTISE!
# ADVERTISE!

---

You can't sell it, if no one knows you have it! I believe the old adage: Advertising doesn't cost, it pays! If you don't spend a little money and make a little effort to advertise, no one will know what you have to sell!

## WHERE TO ADVERTISE

Target your advertising to reach the most people interested in what you have to sell. If car buyers in your area rely heavily on the local auto magazines for car sources, then concentrate most of your advertising there. If you live near a military base, advertise in their publication. If there is a strong ethnic community near you, such as in San Fransico or Miami, then advertise in those ethnic publications. Test different strategies to find out what works best. For example; run a "jumbo" size ad to see how it works compared to a regular size ad. If you have several cars for sale, buy a third or half page and create some interesting ad copy for the space. Here is another idea. Run one short classified ad in the most popular, local paper. Advertise the cheapest car you have. After it is sold, you will still receive calls. Instead of just telling the callers, "the car is already sold," tell them about the other cars you have or about the cars you are about to get.

**Hint:** On a 3x5 index card, enter the date and the callers name and phone number. List the type of vehicle preferred, equipment required and their price range. You can build a tremendous list of potential customers in no time. Every time you make a new purchase, review your list and make some calls for really fast sales!

## FREE ADVERTISING

If you don't have money, or you just want to increase your advertising exposure, try some of these techniques.

**Newspapers:** Some publications will allow you to advertise free; especially those with a small circulation. Call specialty publications such as military newspapers, senior citizens news and so on. Many communities have heritage and ethnic publications that are inexpensive and sometimes free.

**Put a sign in the window:** Whether you drive the car or not, keep at least one sign in the window. Briefly describe the car and print your phone number. Don't include the price. Why? Because you'll get more calls and if the price is not in their budget, you can tell them about your other selections!

**Park it:** Place the car in a highly visible area, preferably where people can easily stop to write down your number. A good location can help you sell several cars each week. If necessary, consider paying a small fee for prime display space. Most property owners will gladly accept your offer.

**Bird Dogs:** Have some business cards printed with your name and phone number. Give some to friends, fellow workers, waitresses and just about everyone you meet. Tell them you sell cars and trucks. Tell them if they send you customers, and if the customer purchases a vehicle from you, you will pay them a $50.00 finders fee. I personally pay $100.00. Tell your "bird dog" to be sure to print their name and phone number on the back of the card before giving it to the customer. Always pay finders fees promptly! I've made thousands of dollars using my bird dog network. After a few months of using the techniques in this book, you will realize you have built a network of sources that continue to pay off time after time.

**Contract Advertising:** Most newspapers and some auto magazines, offer a discount if you advertise on a regular basis. Although, it is not free, in many cases, you can save 25% or more! Talk to a representative of your local publications.

## ADVERTISE TO GET RESULTS

To get fast, effective results, you must advertise creatively. Grab the readers attention, give them the facts, and get them to call. Get excited about what you are selling and you'll write a good ad. Think about the great features your car has and how it will benefit the buyer to own it. Before writing the ad, walk around the car, noting the exterior features. Next, sit inside the car and note the accessories and special features. If the vehicle is economical, then tell them. If the vehicle is inexpensive and therefore will have low monthly payments, then let your customers know. Use adjectives and lots of exclamation points to help describe the car and convey excitement. Here is a typical ad you might see in your local auto magazine:

85 Saab 900 - Automatic, air, stereo, power windows and sunroof. $4,695.00. 555-5612.

Here is another way you could write about the same car:

85 Saab 900 - Must sell now! Factory air, am-fm stereo, cassette, loaded with options including power sunroof! Very Sporty! Great gas mileage! Cheap to own. Low monthly payments. $4,695.00 or best offer. Call Now! 555-5612.

Or how about this:

85 Saab 900 - Guaranteed to be the best quality, lowest priced Saab in town. Call me now for details! 555-5612.

Get the Picture? Although your ad copy will be different from mine, my point is this: You must create interest and motivate people to call at that moment! **Hint:** So that you never miss valuable calls, buy a good telephone answering machine. Be sure to return the calls promptly before your callers buy from someone else!

There are some very good books available on advertising techniques. Just visit your library or bookstore.

# FUNDAMENTALS OF GOOD SALESMANSHIP

### SHOWTIME!

Mr. Brown has called you and would like to see the Toyota Celica you have advertised. Before you hang up, give him clear directions to your house or where the car is located. Tell him to take your phone number with him in case he gets lost.

At this point you should "preview" the car before your customer arrives. Just as a jeweler displays his diamonds as attractively as possible, so should you with your car. Although you have already detailed the car, "freshen" the exterior and interior if needed.

It is also important that the buyer receive a good first impression of you. Buyers of any product often associate the quality of the product with the quality of the salesperson. If your appearance is negative, then Mr. Brown might perceive the car negatively too! Don't take that chance! Practice good salesmanship by having clean hands, clean nails, clean breath and clean clothing. Don't undermine your success by breaking these basic rules.

When Mr. Brown arrives, introduce yourself. A cheerful attitude often relaxes you and your customer. Tell your customer about the car, pointing out extra features and accessories. Know what you are selling! For example, tell Mr. Brown that an article in a recent consumer magazine rated Toyota Celica very highly in reliability and economy. Being prepared is half the battle in any successful venture.

Find out about factory warranties and customer satisfaction of the vehicles you are selling. You can find information like this in car magazines, trade magazines and consumer reports. Find out about it and use it to help you sell! Answer any questions that come up as clearly as you can. For example: Is the mileage correct? If you believe it is (you have a signed odometer statement from the previous owner) then tell your customer it is and that you have a signed odometer statement from the previous owner. What if they ask how long you have you owned the car and why are you selling it? I personally love this question because it gives me an opportunity to sell! Simply tell them you buy cars and trucks for investments and you wholesale to car dealers and also sell directly to the public. By doing this, you bypass the middleman and you can save buyers a lot of money!

Tell your customers that you inspect your cars thoroughly before offering them for sale, and they are welcome to take the car to any mechanic they choose for their own inspection! Tell them you want them to be happy with their car because you would like for them to tell their friends about you. Additionally, you would like to sell them another car sometime in the future! Your honesty will clear the air  of any apprehension they may have and help you make the sale.

It's up to you if they go alone on the test drive or if you go with them. Frankly, it's better if you go because you can show them a good test drive route and also explain any features the car may have. It's also a good time for casual conversation and building trust. Make sure the driver is licensed and is not underage. Don't allow anyone to drive recklessly or abuse your vehicle.

After the test drive, most customers will want to discuss the price. Since you know exactly how much you have invested, you can negotiate to a point where you feel you have made a fair profit. I generally average between $500.00 and $1,000.00 per car. As long as I make a profit, I rarely "kill" a sale because of price. I know I can easily and quickly replace the vehicle I'm selling.

Controlling the final stages of selling often involves overcoming objections, procrastination, fear and a whole rainbow of human emotions. In most cases you will not need to be an expert salesman. If you've prepared the vehicle well and priced it fairly, it will almost sell itself.

Selling and closing technique is another subject altogether. If you feel you would like to improve your selling techniques, then get a copy of one, or all, of these excellent books: Secrets of Closing the Sale, by Zig Zigler, How to Master the Art of Selling, by Tom Hopkins and How to Sell Anything to Anybody, by Joe Girard. Most bookstores and libraries should have a copy.

# COMPLETE

# THE

# PAPERWORK

---

Mr. Brown likes the car and after a little negotiation you both agree on a price. Tell Mr. Brown he should leave a deposit on the car to insure that no one else will buy it. You will need a money receipt book or deposit receipt book. Make sure the receipts are duplicate and preferably carbonless. The receipt should have a line for your customers name, address, phone number and the amount of the deposit. Somewhere on the receipt you should enter the selling price, type of vehicle and the vehicle identification number, commonly referred to as the vin.#. You can get money receipt books at most office supply stores. Give Mr. Brown his copy of the receipt and find out approximately when he'll be coming back to finish the transaction and take the car.

When Mr. Brown returns to take the car, he must pay you in full and complete the paper work. If you are not working with a licensed wholesaler and you do not have a license of your own, then all you need to do is assign the vehicle title to the new owner. You should also complete a "bill of sale" or a purchase order. Most importantly, you should get a signed odometer statement for every transaction. This statement is a federal requirement and is good protection for you and the buyer. These forms can be found at office supply stores and dealer auctions. Print shops can also print them for you. See the Appendix for an illustration of an odometer statement and a bill of sale.

Mr. Brown has signed the forms, received his copies and paid you in full for the car. You have a happy customer because you have sold him a great car far cheaper then he could have bought it anywhere else. Plus, you made a handsome profit for yourself.

He can now take the title to a local license tag office, pay the applicable fees and sales tax (if any) and obtain the new registration. Different states have varying requirements for title and tag transfer and you should check with your state if there is any question about proper transfer.

If you work with a licensed wholesaler, he will explain to you the proper procedure for reassigning titles and purchasing license plates. Most wholesalers will process the title work for you.

If you have decided to obtain your dealers license, you could do all the title processing yourself. For more information on obtaining your license, refer to page 95.

## **FINALLY**

The procedures I've explained in this section are simple and easy to master, although at first glance they may seem foreign. The more you use these techniques, the sharper your skills will become. Don't be intimidated and don't quit before you begin. The rewards are too tremendous to let them get by you!

*"WHAT WE HOPE TO DO WITH EASE, WE MUST FIRST DO WITH DILIGENCE"*

Samuel Johnson

# WHOLESALING

INCLUDES

INTRODUCTION TO WHOLESALING
GETTING STARTED
WHOLESALING, STEP BY STEP
WHOLESALE BUYING AND SELLING
SELLING AT DEALER AUCTIONS
HIRE WHOLESALERS TO WORK FOR YOU
MORE STRATEGIES AND MONEY MAKERS
DRIVE A DREAM CAR - FREE!
FINAL THOUGHTS ON WHOLESALING

# FEW OF US CAN STAND PROSPERITY - ANOTHER MANS, I MEAN.

Mark Twain

# INTRODUCTION TO WHOLESALING

If you think the stock market or investing in real estate is exciting, read this. My local Toyota dealer is having a marathon car and truck sale Friday, Saturday and Sunday. Since I buy and sell to them, I am "on call" to appraise and purchase trade-ins as they arrive. In one day, I'll look at and price more than 30 cars and trucks! Most of them I will buy. As quickly as I buy them and most of the time before I pay for them, I'm on the phone calling other dealers, wholesalers and retail customers. I tell them about the vehicles and the prices I need to get. Making profits anywhere from $100.00 to $500.00, I will sell as many as fifteen cars and trucks in one day. On most of them, I will not spend one penny reconditioning. I simply have my drivers take the car or truck from one dealership to the other! The other dealer gives my driver a bank draft who then brings the draft back to me; that simple, that quick!

Does wholesaling sound exciting to you? Well, you guessed it; *it is exciting and very, very* profitable! Huge volumes of dollars change hands everyday in the wholesaling market-place. Now is the time for you to get started and get your piece of the action.

As with retailing, we will begin as if you do not have any previous knowledge or experience. If you do have experience, you should still review the segments to make sure you haven't missed any techniques that could make you thousands of dollars. Some of the techniques presented here will overlap and can be used for both wholesaling and retailing. As you begin to understand all these techniques, you can combine some of them, thereby increasing your profit potential on both sides. Once you understand all the segments, you'll have created a powerful money machine that will work for you just about anywhere in the world!

# GETTING
# STARTED

---

You can accomplish wholesaling, to some degree, by using some of the techniques in the retail section. For example: You can buy from individuals and then wholesale to dealers. That will work well, but it takes more time and patience. For faster results and bigger profits, I would suggest you try some of the techniques discussed below. To make these techniques work, you should either become an associate of a licensed wholesale dealer or obtain your own license. In 1989, I was wholesaling over 100 cars each month. I had four wholesalers (people just like you) buying and selling full time, not even counting two retail sales representatives. We were selling cars so fast, we could hardly keep up with the paperwork! Sound incredible? It really isn't. It's happening everyday, everywhere in the United States.

## BECOMING A WHOLESALE AGENT

Let's assume you have decided not to get your own license right now, but you would still like to buy and wholesale. You've probably met some wholesalers already, using the sources discussed in retailing. Choose one that you feel comfortable with and explain that you are interested in entering wholesaling and that you have gained some experience while you've been retailing. At some point you should discuss an agreement that would clearly define your association. For example, many wholesalers (myself included) supply everything needed: Dealer plates, insurance, reconditioning, sight drafts and a set line of credit for each associate wholesaler. The only thing my wholesalers paid for, was  gas, tolls and cellular phone bills. We shared the profits and losses on a 60-40 basis. They got 60% of the profits and I got 40%. They, after all, did all the work (actually, it was fun); I supplied everything else. I held in escrow $1,000.00 of their profits in case we had returns or some other problem at a later date. I also had other wholesalers work with me on a flat fee basis. For example, one wholesaler operated with his own money and handled all his own expenses. The only thing he needed from me was use of my license and handling the paperwork. For this, he paid me $100.00 per vehicle; win, loose or draw. If he made a profit of $1,000, he only paid me $100.00 and kept the rest for himself. If he lost money, he still paid me $100.00.

Many licensed wholesalers use a 50-50 split. Discuss with your wholesaler what you would like to do. Work out an agreement that makes both of you happy. Take your time and connect with a wholesaler who has a good reputation. Remember, you will be associated with him and how he conducts business will affect your income.

## GETTING YOUR DEALER LICENSE

At some point, you should consider obtaining a dealer license. In most states, a dealer license and a wholesale license is one in the same. Some states, however, do separate the two. Simply call The Department of Motor

Vehicles, dealer licensing division in your state. If your state separates the two, and has different requirements for each, I would personally obtain the retail dealers license. This license allows you to retail and wholesale. The wholesale dealer license, depending on your state, only allows you to sell to dealers, auctions and other wholesalers. Call The Department of Motor Vehicles in your state and ask them to send you an application for a dealer license. Requirements can vary greatly, but generally they are as follows. You will be required to purchase a dealer bond, issued by an insurance company, which basically assures that you will not commit fraudulent acts against the public. The bond amount varies greatly from state to state. For example, the bond amount required for a California license is $50,000, compared to only $5,000 for Wyoming! This does not mean you actually pay this amount of money. Instead, you pay a yearly premium just like any other insurance policy. The yearly premium is usually very inexpensive; In some states as low as $50.00 per year. You will need a location approved by The Department of Motor Vehicles. An application with information about yourself also will be requested. Some states also require proof of automobile liability insurance.

The cost of becoming licensed is minimal and the advantages are tremendous. The process is not nearly as difficult as many applicants first expect. Be persistent, fill out the forms and you will soon have another very useful tool for investing in the car business.

## SALES TAX EXEMPT

Every vehicle transaction requires the payment and collection of sales tax. The tax varies from state to state but is usually the same amount as a general sales tax. If you are buying a large volume of vehicles this tax could become very costly. To avoid paying this tax, contact the Department of Revenue or Taxation in your state and request a tax exemption or sales tax number. You should apply for the sales tax number at the same time you apply for your dealers license. Not only will you be exempt from sales tax when you purchase vehicles, you also will be exempt from any tax on repairs or improvements to those vehicles.

# OCCASIONS ARE RARE; AND THOSE WHO KNOW HOW TO SEIZE UPON THEM ARE RARER.

Josh Billings

# WHOLESALING STEP BY STEP

---

You've obtained your license or you've made an agreement with a licensed wholesaler. You have some retail experience under your belt and you can't wait to get started. Now all you need is somebody to point you in the right direction! First though, you'll need to know a few more things. All trades and professions use tools and devices to help speed efficiency and productivity. Wholesalers have implemented tools of their own and few could do without them.

## CELLULAR PHONES & BEEPERS

Two tools that will help you immeasurably are the cellular phone and pager/beeper. Both instruments will insure that your wholesale contacts can reach you at all times. For example, once you are a regular wholesaler at ABC Chevrolet, the manager might call you to come look at a recent trade-in. If he can't get in touch with you, he will call somebody else. If you have a phone or a beeper you can talk with him, price the vehicle and ask him to wait for you to get there.

If you buy the vehicle you can, again, reach for your portable phone and quickly sell to another dealer or retail customer. They are also great at auctions for calling other dealers or retail customers when you see a car they might be interested in buying. Phones and beepers come in a variety of styles and price ranges. To get the model that best suites your needs, ask to demo it for a day or so. Many companies also lease cellular phones and beepers.

## SIGHT DRAFTS

Also referred to as bank drafts or simply drafts, these instruments are one of the most important tools of the wholesale and retail trade. Drafts allow you to purchase a vehicle without actually paying for it at the time you take the vehicle. It is a banking instrument similar to a check that amounts to a promise to pay providing the title work is in order.

When you have drafts printed, be sure to include your business name, address and phone number. Also, have printed the name and address of the bank where you would like to have the drafts processed once you have issued them.

Choose any bank you desire to receive and process your drafts. Most banks don't require you to do any other business with them, however, they usually collect a small fee for their services. The fee can vary from $5.00 to $20.00 per transaction, depending on the bank. If you are a good customer, many banks will waive the fee altogether. Since you will soon be making large deposits to your checking account, and therefore a valued customer, ask your bank to waive the draft fee. Does it save much money? Let me put it this way, if you are eventually buying fifty cars per month and the draft fee is $20.00 per draft, that's $1000.00 per month! Try to get the fee waived, and keep the extra $1000.00 for yourself!

When you issue a draft and it arrives at your bank for collection, it will contain the title and any supporting documents such as odometer statements, power of attorney, etc.. Your bank will call you to let you know a draft is in for payment. Most of the time, you will have at least forty-eight hours to come in and examine the draft. If you don't, your bank will return it to the other dealers bank unopened. *This is equivalent to bouncing a check and will seriously affect your credibility! Don't allow it to happen.* Within the time allowed, go to your bank, open the draft and examine the title. If the title is correct, pay the bank for the amount of the draft and keep the title. If the title work has an error or is the wrong title, (it happens) then you can reject it. Your bank will then return it to the selling dealer's bank, with an explanation of why it is being returned unpaid. The selling dealer can then do the necessary corrections and submit the draft again.

On the average, drafts take about ten days to process if the selling dealer has the title present. Often, however, they must pay-off a lien or apply for a duplicate title when a car is traded in. If this happens, the time to process the draft will be much longer. I have had them take as little as five days and as long as six months! During this time, you have possession of the car which allows you time to do any necessary reconditioning and in many cases sell it.

Refer to the appendix and examine the illustration of what a draft should look like. It should be the same size as a standard business envelope. In fact, most drafts are printed on business envelopes with a carbonless insert for you to remove. Keep the insert for your records and as proof of the transaction. Drafts can be printed by your local printer or ordered from large mail-order printing companies. If you are on a tight budget, ask your banker to give you some blank sight drafts. You'll have to print your name and phone number on the face but at least you'll get them free.

## THE DRAFT PROCESS

For a thorough understanding, let's look at a draft transaction from beginning to end. Almost all draft transactions follow this sequence.

1. You locate and purchase a car from Acme Honda.
2. You fill in the blanks on the draft describing the car and I.D.#.
3. Remove the insert and give the draft to the dealer.
4. Acme Honda will give you a purchase order.
5. You can now take the vehicle and leave.

6. Acme's title clerk receives the draft for processing.

7. If the title is present, the clerk does the reassignment and inserts the title inside the draft envelope.

8. The draft is then taken to Acme Honda's bank for deposit.

9. Acme Honda's bank sends the draft to your bank for payment.

10. Upon arrival your bank will call you and give you ample time to come in.

11. You arrive, open the draft, and inspect the title.

12. If correct, you pay the draft with a check, cash or cashiers check and keep the title.

13. If not correct, explain what is wrong and don't pay the draft.

14. Your bank will then return it to Acme Honda's bank

15. Acme Honda's bank will call them with the message.

16. Acme Honda can then correct the title and resubmit it.

17. When it arrives at your bank again, your bank will call you.

18. You examine the title again and pay if it is correct.

Think about what is going on here! If the entire process takes two weeks, you will have two weeks of "float time" which amounts to free time to sell the car to another dealer or retail customer. In fact you can repeat this procedure over and over again, buying and selling before you've paid for the vehicles! You have no cash invested and every opportunity to make a profit before the draft arrives!

If you are using your own money and dealers license, it is easy to understand why the draft process is an important money-making tool. On the other hand, if you have an agreement with a wholesaler, you will use his drafts to purchase vehicles and he will redeem the drafts at his bank. **Hint:** Do not buy recklessly, thinking you have **unlimited** float time to sell before the drafts come in! If you are going to buy a lot of vehicles at one time, be sure you have a place to sell most of them. If not, make sure you have access to money, in case the drafts come in before you sell the vehicles.

# YOU WILL NEVER FIND TIME FOR ANYTHING - IF YOU WANT TIME - YOU MUST MAKE IT.

Charles Buxton

# *WHOLESALE*

## *BUYING & SELLING*

---

If you have a dealer's license or an agreement with a licensed wholesaler, you have all the advantages of retailing and wholesaling combined. This means you can have a few cars for retail and any quantity you feel comfortable with for wholesale. Don't forget to keep an ad running in a car magazine for retail sales.

Where can you find quantities of cars and trucks at wholesale prices and not have to spend days or weeks looking? One of the best places for quantity buying is new-car dealer trade-ins. Go to the new car dealers in your area and ask to see the used car manager or person in charge of wholesaling. Introduce yourself, explain what you do and give him your business card. Your conversation may go something like this: "Hi, my name is John Bower. I'm a wholesaler and I would like to buy any cars or trucks you have available. I also buy aged inventory if you have any." Aged inventory is inventory the dealer has had in stock for a period of time but has not been able to sell. Mr. Manager may say he has nothing today, or he may tell you he does have something and where it is located. He will show you where the keys are located and discuss with you how much he needs to get for each vehicle. If he doesn't give you a price for each vehicle, he may ask you to look them over and make a list of what you're interested in; then he will give you a price. Either way is fine since you will determine on your own what each vehicle is worth.

Next, look the cars over and decide which ones are of interest to you. Drive and inspect each one thoroughly; then list each vehicle on a sheet of paper. Carefully decide each car's wholesale value, factoring in reconditioning cost, including repairs and detailing. Now ask yourself: how much can I sell it for? See page 55 for Condition Checklist and page 59 for Appraising. If necessary, make copies of the pages and carry them with you until you get use to the procedure. These important factors apply whether you are buying one car or one hundred cars. Don't neglect to follow these steps and you will rarely pay too much for any vehicle.

You've made your list. You've driven the vehicles and determined what you feel is a price you can afford to pay and still make a profit when you sell. Now, let's go talk to the used car manager.

Tell Mr. Manager you've looked the cars over and you've decided which ones are of interest to you. You can then discuss each car individually and ask him what he'll take. For example, you have four cars on your list:

1986 Ford Mustang- good condition

1987 Pontiac Firebird- Fair condition

1986 Isuzu Trooper- good condition

1984 Honda Prelude- Fair condition

" Mr. Manager, I am interested in these four vehicles. How much will you take for the '86 Mustang ?" Mr. Manager replies, " I need $2500.00 for that one." You say, "that would be okay, except it needs tires and has a dent in the front fender. Would you take $2100.00?" Mr. Manager might want to negotiate some more or he might say, "O.k., you own it, what's the next one?" You can then continue down the list negotiating and discussing each car individually.

Sometimes, you can use the quantity of cars as a negotiating tool. For example, Mr. Manager might need help getting his appraised value out of the '84 Prelude, but in turn he will give you a great price on the '86 Trooper. In cases like this, as long as your total dollars spent add up to about the same as the total you originally calculated, it really doesn't make any difference if you pay a little more for the Prelude. It's all the same to you and it helps the used car manager save face. In turn, he may help you on future deals.

Let's assume that you were able to agree on the prices for all four vehicles you had listed. Now you must pay for them. If this is the first time you've done business with this dealership, they may want you to fill out an information sheet about you and your dealer license. The information sheet is short and only ask basic information about you and where you bank. You will probably need to supply them with a copy of your dealer's license and sales tax number.

This helps to protect you and them against any fraudulent activity.

Most new car dealers accept drafts since they rarely have the titles present and ready to transfer. Simply fill in the draft with the amount paid and a description of the vehicle. Be sure you get the correct v.i.n. # on the draft. Most dealerships also give you a copy of a purchase order for each vehicle. Additionally, you and Mr. Manager will sign an odometer statement, which is then attached to the title. With each car paid for, tell Mr. Manager it was a pleasure doing business with him and you'll be back very soon!

Depending on how many cars you want to buy, you can continue on to another dealership or you can begin to move the cars you just purchased to reconditioning shops. Better yet, if you know another dealer or retail customer who might be interested in one of the cars, call or take it to them now! If this is one of your first buying trips, consider limiting your purchases until you feel organized and comfortable with what you are doing. So that we can go through each step, we'll assume you are satisfied with the four vehicles you just bought and continue with the process.

Without wasting time, take each vehicle to where it needs to go for repairs or reconditioning. If it needs body work; get it to a body shop immediately. If another car needs tires, get it to the tire store as soon as possible. The point is this: get them ready for resale as quickly as possible. You'll make more money on each car, plus you can go buy more in a shorter period of time!

Now, you've finished reconditioning and the cars are ready to sell. Do you wholesale, retail or both? It really depends on you. Using what you have already learned in the retail portion of this book, call some dealers to find out if they are interested in the vehicles you have for sale. Call the Isuzu dealer, for example, regarding the 1986 Trooper. Call used car dealers you are becoming acquainted with to see if they are interested. Once you build a good network and a good reputation, you'll be able to sell cars and trucks all day long on the telephone! Again, don't forget to keep at least one retail ad running in the newspaper. Don't neglect your retail sales just because you can now wholesale. Your effectiveness as a retailer is stronger then ever since you now have more access and better selection.

# SELLING

## AT

## DEALER AUCTIONS

---

Another option is to take the cars to a dealer auction in your area. If you want to sell fast and have maximum exposure, then you might like this type of selling.

Review dealer auctions on page 42. Since we covered basic information and buying at dealer auctions in this previous section, we will concentrate here on selling at dealer auctions.

If you have not already registered at a dealer auction, call the ones in your area and find out where they are located. Ask how many vehicles are registered each week and how long the auction lasts. If the auctions in your area are small, then you should consider registering at some auctions in larger cities. You will need to register with the auction and provide a copy of your dealer license and bond before you can sell. If you are working with a licensed wholesaler, he will register you to buy and sell under his license. You will receive an auction card with your name and the name of the licensed dealer.

Once you are registered, you can reserve numbers for each of your vehicles. Different auctions have different systems. Generally, you call and ask for a number for each car and truck you intend to run that week. Some auctions will want to list each vehicle individually, using the model and year to determine which lane they will appear in. Some of the larger auctions will not reserve numbers until you bring the vehicles in for registration.

Getting early run numbers usually gives you a better chance of getting more bidders and, therefore, a better price for your vehicles. Some of the best numbers run about an hour after the auction begins. This doesn't mean you won't get a good price for your cars with late numbers; it only means you will probably get a better price with an early number, when more bidders are available. Very late numbers are usually the worst since many buyers have spent their money and left the auction. To help get good numbers, call early or take your vehicles to the auction well in advance of the next sale day. If you become a regular, some auctions reserve their best numbers for their regular dealers and wholesalers.

Now that you have registered and received numbers for your vehicles, make sure they are detailed and ready to sell. On auction day, arrive early enough to inspect your cars and start them. Make sure they are still clean and have the best possible eye appeal.

Since you know exactly what you have invested in each car, it is very easy for you to determine what you can sell it for and still make a profit. Be sure to include auction fees as part of your cost. For example, suppose you have a 1986 Mustang that cost you $2,300.00, including repairs. When the bidding exceeds $2,300.00, you know you're making a profit. Suppose further, the bidding stops at $2,600.00. You now have a profit of $300.00. If you sold all four of the vehicles you brought to this sale, you would make a gross profit of $1,200.00 for the day.

When the auction begins and your cars approach the block, you should be close by so you can represent them. Not all auctions require you to be present at the block. Instead, you tell them prior to the sale, how much you want for the cars and how much they can deviate from that figure.

Once your car is on the block, bidding will begin. Follow the bidding and if you have information about the car which would help it bring more money, then tell the auctioneer so he can announce it. The auctioneer will ask you if the final bid is acceptable. If it is acceptable, tell the auctioneer and sign the selling documents. Represent all of your cars and trucks the same way.

Next, the buyer will drive the car (if it was sold with a drive) and then pay for it. You can either wait to be paid at the auction or the auction can send your payment in the mail. If you do not have the title present, they will pay you with a draft similar to the one you use to pay other dealers and auctions. At the end of the day, add up your profits and get ready to go buy more cars!

It's not unusual for many wholesalers to sell twenty-five or more cars and trucks each week. It's common to expect to receive good numbers from the auctions when you begin selling so many units. And why not? You are making money for the auction and you're also walking away with thousands of dollars of your own!

Since you are already at the auction, you are in a perfect position to look for bargains that may be going through. While waiting for your cars to come to the block, look for repossessions, fleet liquidations and dealers who need cash flow. These sellers will often sell their vehicles at whatever they bring across the block, leaving huge profits for *somebody* at next weeks sale or from your retail customers.

## NO CASH TECHNIQUE

Suppose you see a car that looks good to you. You've started it, looked it over and determined what you think it's worth. Follow the car when it comes to the block. If they announce the title is "not present", that means you have "float time". Often, the auction will even announce approximately how long it will be before you can expect the title. This is great since you do not have to pay for the car until the title comes in! In other words, if you are the successful bidder, you will write a draft for the car. The auction, however, cannot deposit the draft for collection until they have the title! This enables you to either wholesale the car to another dealer (who will give you a draft since you don't have the title) or retail the car for a larger profit. Either way, you'll have nothing invested in an automobile you'll sell for a nice profit!

Here's another technique you'll want to use as you gain experience. Attend an auction, let's say on a Tuesday. Purchase cars and trucks that you know are definite money-makers. (You won't always be successful at this, but experience will certainly help your accuracy!) Next, transfer these cars to another auction in another town. (Ideally, the second auction would be considered the larger and better auction) If you bought the vehicles right and received good numbers, you'll make a considerable profit. Again, you will be selling cars before you've ever paid for them!

## PAYMENT AT AUCTION

When you buy at dealer auctions, you can pay by draft, check or cash. To save more money, consider this: Most auctions charge a draft fee when you pay by draft. This fee varies, depending on the amount you paid for the car, but usually averages around $40.00 per car. To avoid this fee, pay by check. If the title is present, they will deposit your check the very next business day. If the title is not present, they will hold your check until the title arrives. Sometimes this may take only a couple of days, but on the other hand, it's been known to take weeks! Again, you will feel the luxury of "float time" and you'll save the draft fees on all of your purchases. While it's great to save draft fees, don't try this technique unless you know you have the funds to cover you checks. You could lose your auction privileges *and* your excellent reputation.

## WHEN YOU RECEIVE A DRAFT

When you sell a vehicle and do not have the title, you will receive a draft as payment. Keep the draft in a safe place until you receive the title to the vehicle. When you receive the title, reassign it to the buyer, insert it inside the draft and do one of the following. If the car was not sold at auction, call the buyer and tell him you have the title. Tell him you have reassigned it and you would like to deliver the title to him and receive a check. By doing this you get paid much faster and your cash is available to make new purchases. The other way involves depositing the draft at your bank for collection. The draft will then go through the same process outlined on page 103; only this time you are the selling dealer. To help speed up the payment, ask your bank to stamp "Remit Within 48 Hours" on the front of the draft. Better yet, have this printed on the front of the draft when you place your printing order. By doing this, the draft will not remain at the buyer's bank for an indefinite period of time. You should also ask your bank to give immediate credit to your checking account for sight drafts. Most banks will accommodate you, especially after you have established a good relationship.

### SELL TO OTHER DEALERS

One of the great things about wholesaling, is you are never locked into a certain vehicle. Whether it's a retail buyer, another dealer or an auction, there is always a buyer somewhere ready, willing and able to make the purchase.

Assuming you have bought the four vehicles in the foregoing example, and you don't have an auction to attend, what are the alternatives for a quick sale? One of the quickest ways to sell is to other dealers. Retail dealers are always looking for good, clean vehicles for their inventory. You'll need to decide whether to recondition them first or sell them just the way you bought them. I personally prefer to detail my vehicles first, since first impressions or "eye appeal" is very important to making the sale. In fact, many new car dealers want the car "front line ready", before they'll agree to purchase. Front line ready means the car is *ready both mechanically and in appearance.* All he has to do is park the car on his front line and sell it.

Get acquainted with the used car managers in your area. Find out what kind of inventory they like to buy. When you are out buying, you will then know which dealer is most likely to be interested in buying a certain car or truck. Often, you can just call and tell them about the car even before you buy it. If it's a small profit, and you can sell the car before you buy it, great! If you can't sell it quickly on the phone, then you might want to skip this one and move on to the next one. You'll avoid tying up your money for a small profit. **Remember this:** Retail dealers buy a lot of vehicles. They have to buy these cars and trucks from someone and it may as well be from you.

## MULTIPLE STATE AUCTIONS

Another way to build profits quickly is to sell auction to auction, from one state to another. Since I enjoy traveling, this method works great for me. For example, if I want to spend some time in Southern California, I'll attend an auction there and perhaps buy four wheel drive trucks and vans. Since I plan on taking them to a northern climate, I try to buy vehicles without air conditioning, knowing I can buy them cheaper here, where the weather is quite warm. I can then transport them to Seattle or another northern city. While those vehicles are being transported, I might stop in Phoenix or Las Vegas and buy additional vehicles. Once I arrive in Seattle, I can sell the vehicles to individual dealers or send them to another auction. One dealer license is all you need to register and do business on a wholesale basis. From Seattle, I might decide to go to Vancouver, British Columbia, which is only a few scenic hours away. While there, I might talk to dealers or individuals interested in buying cars or trucks. I'll give them my card and tell them to contact me when they are ready to buy. All along the way, I am building a network of buyers and sellers who will call me from time to time to buy or sell cars or trucks.

You should not begin multiple state buying and selling until you've grown accustomed to all of the techniques and methods we have discussed. Transportation costs, auction fees, lodging and other cost should be factored into your total cost of the vehicles. If you are only buying one or two vehicles, it may not be the best way to make maximum profits. On the other hand, if you are just wanting to take a free vacation, a few cars or trucks should cover most of the cost. If you decide to try multiple state wholesaling, begin by buying and selling at auctions within your state and then expand into bordering states.

# THERE'S ONLY ONE THING THAT MONEY WON'T BUY AND THAT'S POVERTY.

Joe E. Lewis

# HIRE
# WHOLESALERS
## TO WORK FOR YOU

---

Another alternative worth consideration, is to hire wholesalers to work for you. If you are too busy or you are just not interested in spending your own time getting out and locating vehicles to buy and sell, you can hire other people to do it for you.

Once you've obtained your dealer license, talk to other wholesalers and ask them to refer people they know who are experienced wholesalers. When you are contacted, explain your program and guidelines. For example, your guidelines may look something like this:

1. Buying limit: $50,000.00. No single purchase over
   $10,000.00 unless presold.

2. 50-50 profit and loss split.
3. 50-50 sharing of expenses.(excluding cellular phones etc.)
4. No vehicles to be held more than 14 days.
5. Daily summary of activity, i.e. units bought and sold.
6. All paper work turned in immediately.
7. Commissions paid weekly.
8. Vehicles held in inventory more than 14 days will be devalued $____ and charged against commissions.

The agreement can be as long or as short as you like. You should, however, definitely have a written agreement signed by both parties. You should also do a little background check to make sure your wholesalers are of good character.

The cash flow and profits here can be tremendous. Just think: if each wholesaler working for you only makes a profit of $2000.00 per week; that means you get $1000.00 per week. Multiply that by the number of wholesalers working for you and you can easily see the results!

It is important that you have adequate working capital to cover all the drafts that will be issued; even though most of the vehicles will be sold before the drafts arrive for payment. Talk to your banker or an investor about increasing your working capital. Another alternative is keep it simple for awhile; retailing and wholesaling by yourself. You'll be amazed how quickly your working capital will increase.

*A MAN CAN FAIL MANY
TIMES, BUT HE ISN'T
A FAILURE UNTIL HE
BEGINS TO BLAME
SOMEBODY ELSE.*

John Burroughs

# MORE
# STRATEGIES
# &
# MONEY MAKERS

---

For this writer, the methods we have already discussed are the most successful and reliable. I have used them day in and day out for years with proven results. More radical methods which other wholesalers use successfully include buying and selling insurance recoveries, grey market vehicles, and "red lite" vehicles.

## INSURANCE RECOVERIES

These are vehicles that have been wrecked, fire damaged, water damaged or stolen and recovered. Insurance companies, after paying off the claims of their insured customers, liquidate these vehicles for what they can get at salvage vehicle auctions. To find out where these auctions are held, call automobile insurance companies and ask which auctions they use to sell their salvage vehicles.

## GREY MARKET VEHICLES

Grey market vehicles consist mostly of cars that have been manufactured in other countries and not intended for use in the United States. They usually consist of upper end luxury and sports cars such as Porsche, Mercedes, Jaguar, Lamborghini and Farrari.

Most of these cars entered the United States in the early and mid-nineteen eighties. At that time, the U.S. dollar was very strong against other foreign currencies, thereby, making imported cars very inexpensive in terms of U.S. dollars. Currency exchange and fluctuations will be discussed further in the exporting section off this book. For now, suffice it to say that grey market cars were shipped to the U.S. from other countries such as England, Germany and Italy. They were then modified to meet U.S. safety and polution standards and then sold to car dealers and to the public.

For various reasons, these cars fell out of favor with buyers, luxury car dealers and bankers. Some of the reasons include availability of parts and service, warranty obligations and by-passing the North American distributor and franchise dealerships. Franchise dealers profits were severely diminished and many refused to service these vehicles. Bankers became concerned about the new imports because the franchise dealers who they bank rolled could not sell their inventory when the grey market twin was selling for up to twenty-five percent less! These problems, along with a change in the value of U.S. dollars abroad, made the grey market dwindle rapidly. Consequently, since the availability of service and bank financing is lacking, these cars are bringing considerably less than their manufactured for the U.S. counterpart.

## RED LIGHT VEHICLES

Most dealer auctions will have some vehicles that cross the block under the red light. This means, the vehicle is sold "as is" and may have serious mechanical or structural problems. It could have, for example, frame damage, water damage, engine or transmission problems. With few exceptions, if you are the high bidder under the red light, you own the vehicle regardless of the problems it may have. If you are going to buy red light vehicles, stick to fleet sales, bank repo's and liquidations. These larger companies and banks often sell their vehicles under the red light, regardless of the condition, which means you can often get good vehicles at discounted prices. The best way to be safe is to look the cars over thoroughly before they come to the block.

## T.M.U.'S

These vehicles have true miles unknown, hence the abbreviation "T.M.U.". Anyone selling a car or truck, whether a dealer or an individual, must disclose if the miles are correct. If the odometer is in excess of its mechanical limits, has been replaced or is not correct for any reason, then it must be disclosed as true miles unknown. T.M.U can greatly affect what a car is worth; especially late model vehicles. New car dealers and many individuals will not buy vehicles with incorrect mileage.

## ODOMETER DISCLOSURE

Never be tempted to let someone alter the odometer reading on any car you own. Never buy a vehicle that you know has altered mileage. There are federal and state laws with severe penalties for anyone convicted of this crime! If you have followed my guidelines you will never need to alter mileage to make a profit. It's too dangerous and it isn't necessary. For your protection, always get a signed odometer statement for every car you purchase and sell.

# IF YOU WANT A BETTER PERSPECTIVE, YOU MUST FIRST MOVE TO HIGHER GROUND.

Chinese Proverb

# DRIVE
# A
# "DREAM CAR"
# FREE!

---

I drive any car I want, anytime I want and I haven't had a car payment in sixteen years! Over this time, I have owned just about every kind of vehicle you can think of: Porsche, Mercedes, Lotus, Jaguar and many more. Too good to be true? Of course not, if you know how to make the system work for you.

If you could rent a Corvette, Mercedes, or Porsche, how much would it cost per day. Maybe $100.00, maybe even more? If you rented it for three or four weeks, it could cost $3000.00 or more. Either way is very costly and a waste of a precious resource: **Your working capital!**

The following technique may have already occurred to you if you are already retailing and wholesaling. This technique should be used cautiously if you are operating on a limited budget. Although you should sell the car before the draft is presented for payment, be prepared to pay the draft when it arrives, either with your own funds or borrowed funds. To get a clearer understanding of the technique, let's walk through it step by step.

The first step to a dream car that cost you nothing is to locate a car that is of interest to you. Look for exotics at luxury new car dealers such as Mercedes, Jaguar, and Cadillac. Talk to the used car manager and find out what he has to wholesale. A Mercedes dealer, for example, may not want to keep a Jaguar on his lot and therefore be willing to wholesale it. Many of the new car dealers you already do business with will receive exotics in trade. Make sure they know to call you whenever one comes in.

Since you are looking for "float time", casually ask the manager if the title is in yet. If it is, you will have about a week to ten days before your draft is deposited and is presented at your bank for collection.

More often, exotics and luxury cars have prior financing and, therefore, a lien on the title. When it is traded in the lien must be paid off. A check must be issued to the lienholder and then mailed. Large dealerships can take weeks just to get this completed. Once the check is received, the lienholder will satisfy the lien and mail the satisfaction notice or title back to the dealer. During this entire process you have received several weeks and sometimes, several months of float time. If the lienholder is out of state, you will receive even more float time. I once purchased a BMW that took almost six months to receive a title. During that time, I drove the car free of payments and free of interest!

Dealer auctions are another good source for exotics with float time. Before bidding, look at the light system to find out if the title is present. Most auctions have a light (usually blue) to indicate if the title is present. If the blue light is on, the title is not present. Additionally, many auctioneers or sellers announce how long the title might be delayed. In fact, some auctions allow the buyer to return a car if the title is not presented within a certain number of weeks. Most buyers choose not to return the car, especially if they're happy with it or have already sold it. If you are the successful bidder on a dream car with no title present, pay the auction with a sight draft. This way, you'll have the "no title present float time" and the "draft float time," thereby extending your total float time considerably.

Let's summarize what is taking place here. You receive an exotic car purchased with a draft. You intentionally bought the car knowing the title is not yet available for transfer to you. Consequently, you do not have to use any of your working capital until the title has arrived and your draft is presented for payment.

The exotic will be yours absolutely free of any payments or interest. This will continue until you redeem the draft, which in most cases will take several weeks to several months. During this time, you can drive and enjoy the car and in many cases, sell it for a considerable profit. There is no interest to pay, no payments and an opportunity to make a nice profit! This is as close as it gets to getting paid to drive a car you've always dreamed about!

Buy any car you want as long as you buy it at wholesale or less. Drive it, enjoy it and then sell it for a profit. Then, buy another car you've always wanted and do the same thing all over again! Never again waste your money on car payments! Never again watch your car become worth less and less each year!

# FINAL

# THOUGHTS

# ON

# WHOLESALING

Once you become familiar with the automobile business and use the techniques outlined here, wholesaling will seem so easy you'll wonder why you never thought of it before. As with most things worth doing, it is ***getting started and staying with it*** that is most difficult.

In the beginning, you may feel uncomfortable and unsure of yourself. Don't let this discourage you. Everybody in this business, at one time or another, was new and inexperienced.

Make progress one step at a time and weigh what you do before you do it. Buy and sell vehicles, keeping in mind your eventual goal of financial freedom.

Lastly, the profits will begin to roll in. You may make more money than you ever imagined. Make a commitment to save at least half of your profits to reinvest and expand your new business.

# EXPORTING

INCLUDES

INTRODUCTION TO EXPORTING
CURRENCY EXCHANGE
WHERE TO SELL
HOW TO SELL
SHIPPING & CUSTOMS
GETTING PAID
FINAL THOUGHTS

# *INTRODUCTION TO EXPORTING*

---

Imagine this: It's 1983 and the prosperous eighties are just beginning to bear fruit. The economy is rolling forward at a seemingly unstoppable pace. As a result, the U.S. dollar is gaining value world-wide. This in turn makes foreign products of all types' cheaper to American consumers.

For car buyers, especially luxury car buyers, new options become available. You could either buy your luxury or sports car at a local dealership and pay the current market price in U.S. dollars or, since the dollar is so strong, you could go directly to the country of origin, exchange dollars for the local currency and receive a whopping discount. For example, a Mercedes or Jaguar costing $32,000.00 in the U.S. could easily be purchased for $24,000.00 in Europe; you save $8,000.00!

It's easy to understand why so many wholesalers, myself included, jumped into the import-export market. It might cost you $1,000.00 to $1,800.00 to ship the car and bring it up to U.S. specifications. You could then easily price the car three or four thousand less than the going U.S. market value and still make a profit of $2,000.00 to $3,000.00 on each unit. Many times you could make $5,000.00 or more on one vehicle!

I remember my first import-export experience. It was 1984 and I was doing extremely well retailing and wholesaling using the methods outlined in parts 1 and 2 of this book. By that time, a friend of mine had been importing for well over a year. He helped me to understand the process and to gain my first contacts in Europe.

After pricing dozens of vehicles, I selected a 1984 Porsche Carrera as my first European investment. We purchased the car from a dealer in London and shipped it to Houston, Texas. The Porsche was then modified to meet

U.S. safety and E.P.A. emissions standards. Since this was my first exotic car, I decided to enjoy it for awhile. Approximately six months later, I sold the car and made a $3,000.00 profit! Imagine driving an exotic car for six months and then making money when you sell it! It was like getting paid to drive a car that you normally only dream about.

For the next few years, importing remained an important source for wholesalers and importers. During the same time, U.S. luxury and sports car franchise dealers were feeling the impact these "grey market" imports were having on them. Eventually, the U.S. economy began to flatten and the dollar gradually decreased in value. With a few exceptions such as Lamborghini, Ferrari and collectibles, direct importing no longer paid big dividends. The weaker dollar, however, paved the way for another opportunity; exporting.

# CURRENCY
# EXCHANGE

---

Almost every country uses its' own form of currency for buying and selling goods and services. The currency of each country fluctuates on a daily basis against other currencies depending on factors such as inflation, recession, interest rates, world peace, speculation and numerous other factors.

Without delving too deeply into the mechanics of foreign exchange, suffice it to say that, if the dollar is strong, then it is time to import. A strong dollar allows a person with U.S. dollars to buy more foreign goods for the same amount of money. Conversely, when the dollar is weak, foreign buyers can buy more U.S. goods for the same amount of money with their currency.

To illustrate, suppose the U.S. dollar and the German mark have been trading at about the same level for many years; let's say 1 U.S. dollar = 1.8 German marks (DM). Say your in the market for a German clock. After pricing German clocks in U.S. stores, you determine the price is averaging $150.00. On a vacation to Germany, you see the same clock in a German store priced at 180 DM. Using your calculator and the exchange rate, you determine a whopping savings of 33% over the identical clock back home!

Exchange Rate: $1.00 = 1.8 DM

German Price : 180 DM

Converted to U.S.$ : 180DM/1.8 = $100.00

In other words, you pay only $100.00 for the clock because you were smart enough to exchange currencies. Suppose the exchange rate changes before you buy the clock. The rate now becomes 2 DM for $1.00. You will save even more money!

Exchange Rate: $1.00 = 2 DM

Price of Clock: 180 DM

Converted to U.S.$: 180/2 DM = $90.00

At this exchange rate, the clock will only cost you $90.00 U.S.!

On the other hand, let's say you are in Germany and the value of the dollar begins to slip. Suddenly, everything begins to cost more for you because you hold U.S. dollars. You call some banks and determine the exchange rate is now only 1.5 DM to the dollar! You rush over to the clock store and see the clock is still priced at 180 DM. Using your calculator you determine the same clock, at the same store, at the same price (German marks), will now cost you $120.00 in U.S. dollars! At this price you are really are not going to save much over the one back in the United States. Now you must decide whether to wait and hope the dollar rebounds in value or buy now before it weakens even more.

On the other side of the preceding example, German tourist in the U.S. would be enjoying a stronger German mark as the dollar waned in value. They could then exchange their marks for more dollars and therefore more buying power. As you can see, currency value and fluctuations determine the feasibility of both importing and exporting.

The preceding example brings us to where we are today. The German mark and most other currencies are relatively strong against the U.S. dollar. Hence, foreign buyers can buy U.S. goods such as cars and trucks at tremendous discounts.

## FLOATING OR LOCKED RATE

When you begin to export to Europe, Canada and other parts of the world, you will at some point be asked to lock a rate or to let the rate float.

If you lock a rate, you are committing to your buyer that you will accept an exchange rate equivalent to what it is at the present time. For example, suppose the exchange rate is 1.5 marks to the dollar and you sell a Corvette for $20,000.00. The Corvette, by the way, cost you $18,000.00. Converting to German marks, the car would cost your buyer 30,000 marks. By locking in, when the buyer pays you, he will give you 30,000 marks. Sounds fine, right? It really depends on what happens to the exchange rate and when he pays you. Suppose you agree to accept full payment when the car arrives. Three weeks pass, the car arrives and you receive payment of 30,000 marks (1.5 x 20,000= 30,000). You go to the bank to convert the marks and discover the rate has changed in the three weeks since you made the deal. The rate is now 1.7 marks to the dollar. You agree to the exchange and much to your surprise, you only get $17,647.00! The value of the mark decreased and cost you $2,353.00 on just one car! To summarize; three weeks ago, you could have given the bank 1.5 marks to receive $1.00. Now you must give the bank 1.7 marks to receive $1.00. This is a change in value of almost 12%.

On the other hand, if the exchange rate goes the other way and the dollar is now worth 1.4 marks, then you'll make more profit than you expected. Going to the same bank when the exchange rate is 1.4 marks will give you $21,428.00; an additional profit of $1,428.00!

Should you lock in? It depends on how soon you get paid, how well you understand the currency market and if you are a bit of a speculator. If you get paid within days after the agreement, then you usually don't have to be concerned. If you must wait two or three weeks while the car is being shipped, then locking in can put you on the edge of your seat. You should also factor in the current exchange rate. Is it low or high? Does it seem to come back to an average exchange? If the exchange rate is already low, you can be fairly confident that it is going to go back up. Consequently, locking in a rate can cost you some serious money.

## FLOATING RATE

Using this method you and the buyer agree on a price in U.S. dollars. You must be paid at the prevailing exchange rate when the car is shipped or delivered. Using this method, you are assured you will get $20,000.00 worth of German marks regardless of the exchange rate at the time of the sale.

When you get paid, you and the buyer simply take the selling price ($20,000.00) and multiply it by the current exchange rate. Now you have in German marks, an amount equivalent to $20,000.00. You can now go to any bank and exchange the marks for dollars. While you will not make a larger profit than expected, you will be assured of getting enough marks to convert to $20,000.00. In this way, you will always know exactly how much profit you can expect to make.

# WHERE
# TO
# SELL

---

There are more than 194 countries throughout the world. The private and public sectors of almost all these countries require cars and trucks. Since only a handful manufacture their own, most vehicles are imported.

Kuwait, for example, is one of the wealthiest countries in the world. They do not, however, manufacture their own cars and trucks. During the occupation of Kuwait by Irag, over 300,000 vehicles were lost! Family cars, police cars, ambulances, trucks and more were stolen or completely destroyed by the Iragi armies.

When the war ended, Kuwait began immediately to acquire vehicles as quickly as possible. Three hundred Chevrolet Caprices were bought in a single day to partially equip the Kuwait City Police Department. The citizens of Kuwait also shopped anxiously for cars and trucks to replace their stolen and destroyed vehicles. U.S. made cars and trucks were and still are at this writing in strong demand.

Since almost all countries need to acquire vehicles of all types, the answer to where you sell really depends on where you prefer to work and travel. What's more, you don't have to limit your exports to just one country or region. In making your decision about where to sell, factor in the duty rate, taxes, stability of the local currency, shipping cost and for how much and how quickly you can sell. Refer to the Appendix to contact the countries embassy or consulate for the most recent requirements.

Assuming that you are a U.S. or Canadian wholesaler and this is your first export venture, you might consider exporting to some of the easier countries first. Canada, for example, adjoins the U.S. and you can enter without a passport. Transporting your vehicles will be by land, thereby allowing you to easily handle any problems that may develop. You can, if you want, literally drive the vehicle to its' destination.

For a first time venture to Europe, I would recommend Germany. Most Germans speak English, the economy is much like the U.S. and there are many enterprising wholesale and retail dealers who are interested in what you have to sell. In fact, some U.S. dealers are opening their own dealerships in the larger cities.

For the Middle East, I would recommend Kuwait. The citizens are friendly, they are in the process of rebuilding their country and they like almost anything American. Better yet, the duty is only 4% and there is no value added tax. Again, you should have a contact before you ship.

One of the most exciting and enjoyable ways to determine where to sell is get a world map and select countries that appeal to you. Next call the embassy or consulate of the countries and explain that you are interested in exporting cars and trucks. They will explain to you any requirements as well as applicable duties and taxes. You can also contact the chamber of commerce of the countries that interest you. Ask the chamber to send you a recent newspaper. Be sure it includes the classified sections.

Many countries maintain groups and organizations here in the U.S. The consulate or your local library can probably give you their addresses and telephone numbers. These groups can sometimes give you valuable information and contacts. Who knows, one of the members may have a relative or friend who needs to buy a car!

Next, you should probably visit the country. With few exceptions, you will need a passport. Go to your local post office and pick up a passport application well in advance of your trip. Visit the major cities and stay at a hotel that employs locals who speak fluent English.

Most hotel employees will be glad to answer your questions and assist you in getting answers to questions. They can tell you where helpful information can be found as well as where local auto dealers are located. They can often tell you which cars are most popular and other important factors. If necessary, hotel employees can act as a translator for you and a potential buyer.

On one of my first trips to Germany, I stayed at the Frankfurt Intercontinental Hotel. A hotel employee typed a letter of introduction for me (in German of course), explaining in the letter who I was and that I was in Frankfurt gathering orders for a later shipment. Since the characters on a German typewriter and a U.S. typewriter are different, this assistance became quite valuable. I made copies of the letter and left a copy with every dealer I visited.

Lastly, you should look for unusual opportunities throughout the world. Listen to the news and read papers to ascertain if events anywhere in the world could have an effect on the demand for cars and trucks. If you think it might, then contact the consulate of the affected country or the United States Department of Commerce. Some enterprising individual or company is going to meet the demand. It may as well be you!

## DESTINATION: CANADA

Exporting cars and trucks to Canada is growing rapidly. The Free Trade Agreement between Canada and The United States is gradually eliminating the duty and standardizing safety requirements on motor vehicles of U.S. and Canadian origin.

For our Canadian investors, we have included a special update for exporting/importing to Canada. If you are a Canadian citizen or a U.S. wholesaler preparing to export/import to Canada, review the following customs requirements and Transport Canada's Motor Vehicle Safety Act requirements. At first glance, these requirements may seem intimidating. In reality, the requirements are minimal and most Canadian officials are very helpful and supportive.

Two departments determine what is eligible for entry into Canada: Revenue Canada Customs and Excise and Transport Canada, which deals with safety requirements. Certain vehicles may meet the requirements of Revenue Canada, customs and excise legislation, but the same vehicle may not meet the requirements of Transport Canada's Motor Vehicle Safety Act.

The Motor Vehicle Safety Act requires that all vehicles imported into Canada comply with the Canada Motor vehicle Safety Standards (CMVSS) in effect on the date the vehicle was manufactured. All vehicles must meet these standards **except**:

* Vehicles, other than buses, manufactured at least 15 years before the date of importation. These vehicles need not meet any safety standards.

* Vehicles being used temporarily by visitors or tourist.

* Vehicles in transit through Canada to another destination.

Vehicles not manufactured for retail sale in Canada or The United States do not meet the importation requirements and are not eligible for importation into Canada.

A vehicle manufactured for Canada or The United States retail market will bear a Statement of Compliance label (SOC) which states the vehicle conforms to all applicable federal motor vehicle safety standards in effect on the date of its' manufacture. Any vehicle with this certification will be treated as if it is being imported from The United States. All customs offices have a Declaration of Importation which must be completed by the importer.

If a vehicle does not bear the compliance label, the only legal means of certifying compliance, at this time, is to contact the manufacturer and obtain a written statement that the vehicle complies. Dealers, garages, mechanics and compliance companies at the time of this writing, are not authorized to certify compliance. A non-complying vehicle will not be allowed entry into Canada on a permanent basis. Proposed amendments to the Canadian Motor Vehicle Safety Act would allow most U.S. certified vehicles to be imported and then modified by someone other than the manufacturer. These changes may occur in late 1991.

Under the Free Trade Agreement between Canada and The United States, vehicles four years old or older as of 1991 will be allowed into Canada provided the vehicle bears a statement of compliance label attached by the manufacturer. This label must state the vehicle complies with all applicable United States Federal Motor Vehicle Safety Standards. This label is usually secured on the drivers side door frame or post. Other times it may be on the drivers side of the instrument panel.

The importer/exporter must also insure that Canada's metric system requirements are met. If the speedometer is not already calibrated in kilometers, then the importer can simply purchase the required adhesive label from the Canadian Automobile Association or other supplier of auto accessories.

These vehicles must also meet additional certification that they comply with Canadian Safety Standards regarding restraint systems and bumpers. The vehicles listed below have been certified by the manufacturers as meeting bumper and seat belt anchorage standards of Canada (CMVSS 215 & CMVSS 210).

For vehicles not on the list, the importer/exporter must obtain a letter from the manufacturer stating compliance with Canadian bumper and seat belt standards. If a letter is not obtainable, then the vehicle is not eligible for registration in Canada. This list is updated as more manufacturers submit information. For the latest information contact: Transport Canada Vehicle Importation

13th. Floor, Canada Building
344 Slater Street
Ottawa, Ontario, K1A ON5
Telephone: 613-998-2174

## PASSENGER CARS FOUR YEARS OLD OR OLDER PERMITTED FOR IMPORTATION FROM THE UNITED STATES

**** Vehicles 15 years or older are exempt from the Motor Vehicle Safety Act requirements.
**** All models less than 15 years old up to and including 1984 model years.

### ALFA ROMEO

All 1985 to 1988 Spider models.
All 1985 & 1986 GTV-6 models.
No 1987 Milano models are eligible.

## BMW

All 1985 to 1988 models.

## PLYMOUTH

1985 to 1988 Horizon & Horizon SE (4dr.)

1985 to 1988 Gran Fury Salon

1985 to 1988 Colt 2dr.

1986 to 1988 Colt 4dr.

1988 Colt Vista

## DODGE

1985 to 1988 Omni & Omni SE (4dr.)

1985 to 1988 Diplomat Salon & Salon SE

!985 & 1986 Dodge 600 Convertible

1985 to 1988 Colt 2dr.

1985 to 1988 Colt 4dr.

1988 Colt Vista

1988 Dynasty & Dynasty SE

1985 to 1988 Newport

1985 to 1988 Fifth Avenue (RWD)

1985 & 1986 Chrysler Limousine

1985 to 1988 Lebaron Convertible

1988 New Yorker & New Yorker Landau (FWD)

## RENAULT

1985 & 1986 Sport Wagon All

1985 & 1986 Fuego All

1988 Medallion All

## AMC

1985 to 1987 Alliance 2dr., 4dr. & Convertible

1985 to 1987 Encore 2dr. and 4dr.

## FORD

All 1985 to 1988 models.

## GENERAL MOTORS

All 1985 to 1988 models except:

 1985 Pontiac 6000 wagon

 1985 Pontiac Firebird

 1985-86 Chevrolet Sprint

 1985-86 Chevrolet Spectrum

## HONDA/ACURA

All 1985 to 1988 models except:

 1985 to 1988 CRX HF

 1985 CRX

 1985 Civic

## HYUNDAI

All  1986 Excels

All  1987 Excels except with passive restraint system.

## JAGUAR

All  1985 to 1988 models.

## MAZDA

All  1985 to 1987 models except:

1986 & 1987 RX7 models

1987 626 with passive restraint system

## MERCEDES-BENZ

All  1985 to 1987 models.

## NISSAN

All  1985 to 1987 models.

1988 Infiniti Q45

1988 Sentra wagon B12

All other 1988 Nissan cars can not be imported.

## ROLLS-ROYCE/BENTLEY

All  1985 to 1987 models.

## SUBARU

All 1985 or 1986 models **can not** be imported.

All 1987 models can be imported except:

Justy

L series hatchback

L series 3 door models.

## TOYOTA

All 1985 to 1987 models except:

1985-86-87 Corolla FX

## VOLKSWAGEN/AUDI/PORSCHE

All 1985 to 1987 models except:

1985 to 1987 Audi 5000 models

1985 to 1987 Audi 4000, Coupe GT, Quattro

## VOLVO

All 1985 to 1988 models.

Contact Transport Canada for updates to this list.

If the Canadian Motor Vehicle Safety Standards Act is amended in late 1991, part of the amendment will allow safety standards modifications by someone other than the manufacturer. The allowable areas of modification may include:

* Bumper standards (CMVSS 215)
* Metric speedometer requirement
* Tether anchorage requirement (210.1)
* Daytime running lights (CMVSS 108).

No modification will be allowed to the restraint system. If it does not already comply, the vehicle can not be imported.

Following is a summary of information regarding automobile exporting/importing from the United States to Canada.

* * Vehicles 15 years old or older need not meet any motor vehicle safety regulations. They must be 15 years old or older by month and year of manufacture.

* * 1977 to 1984 models must bear the manufacturer's U.S. compliance label and the exporter/importer must insure that the speedometer can be read in metric.

* * 1985 1986, and 1987 (accommodating the four year old or older requirement of customs legislation) models must bear the manufacturers U.S. compliance label, have no outstanding recalls and meet Canada motor vehicle safety

168

standards by way of Transport Canada's permitted list as shown on previous pages. The exporter/importer must also insure that the speedometer can be read in metric.

\* \* 1988 and 1989 model year vehicles manufactured prior to December 1, 1989 must meet all the same requirements as 1985, 1986 and 1987 models outlined above. This is applicable to immigrants and returning residents only.

\* \* Vehicles manufactured in **December 1989 or later** (most 1990 and all 1991 model year vehicles) to meet U.S. Federal Motor Vehicle Safety Standards **do not** comply with Canadian Motor Vehicle Safety Standards. Unless the manufacturer can certify the vehicle to meet all applicable Canadian Motor Vehicle Safety Standards, the vehicle is not eligible for importation into Canada.

\* \* Current model year (1991) U.S. complying vehicles do not meet Canadian Motor Vehicle Safety Standards and are **not eligible** for importation unless the manufacturer certifies the vehicle meets all Canadian Motor Vehicle Safety Standards.

You should contact Transport Canada on a regular basis to obtain updates to these requirements.

## CANADIAN DUTIES AND TAXES

If your vehicle complies with the requirements as outlined on the previous pages, in most cases you will be required to pay duty and taxes. When your vehicle arrives at customs, you will be asked for proof of ownership and a bill of sale stating how much you paid for the vehicle. Duty and taxes will be calculated based on the price on your bill of sale.

To calculate duty and taxes on vehicles of U.S. origin: U.S. price x the exchange rate = Canadian value.

+ Duty   6.4%

+ G.S.T. 7.0%

+ Excise tax ($100.00 in-dash air conditioning)

= Total Duty and Taxes

To illustrate, suppose you are exporting/importing a Porsche 928. You paid $14,000 in U.S. dollars.

$14,000.00 x exchange rate (1.17)= $16,380.00

x Duty Rate 6.4%          = $ 1,048.32

x Goods/Services Tax (G.S.T.) 7% = $ 1,219.98

+ Excise Tax (air conditioning) = $   100.00

= Total Amount Due ************** $ 2,368.30

If the vehicle was not manufactured in the United States or Canada, the rate of duty will be 9.2%.

You may be asked to pay duty at the 9.2% rate if you are exporting /importing for commercial purposes. If you are shipping several vehicles at the same time and the bill of sale for each vehicle has the same name or a company name as the owner, then customs might assume the vehicles are for commercial purposes and apply the 9.2% rate of duty. If the bill of sale for each vehicle has a different name as the owner, then customs will apply the 6.2% rate.

Customs will usually look at each case individually in determining which rate to apply. For example, four vehicles arrive at customs and the bill of sale has the same owners name for all four vehicles. The owner explains to customs that he is a car collector or that the cars are intended for use by his entire family. Customs will usually give the benefit of the doubt to the owner and apply the lower duty of 6.4%.

Before you ship to Canada, especially your first time, call your local customs office. Ask them to calculate duty and taxes on the vehicle you intend to import.

**REVENUE CANADA, CUSTOMS AND EXCISE**
**IMPORT AND EXPORT CONTROL**
**5TH. FLOOR, CONNAUGHT BUILDING**
**OTTAWA, ONTARIO**
**K1A ON5**
**TELEPHONE 613-954-7209**

## CANADIAN DEALER LICENSING

Obtaining a dealer license in Canada is a relatively easy process. Requirements and fees vary slightly from province to province. Generally, you will need an office location and an occupational permit approved by your city or district, a registration fee and in some provinces, you will pay a fee to a compensation fund. To receive an application and more information contact Consumer and Commercial Relations of Canada located in your province.

# HOW

# TO

# SELL

---

Now that you know the fundamentals, how do you reach individuals and dealers in foreign countries that are interested in what you have to offer? For the first time exporter without contacts, one of the best ways to start immediately is to go to the country that interest you. Determine the feasibility of exporting to this country by

173

calling the consulate, trade organizations and The United States Department of Commerce.

Next, put together a catalog of cars and trucks that is representative of the types of vehicles you can purchase. A loose leaf notebook will work well. Pack the catalog with as many pictures of as many vehicles as possible. Lay-out a page with two or three photographs to a page. Underneath each photograph, type a description of the vehicle including the year, make, model and the asking price. Use color photographs and paste each one to the page or go to a printer with a color laser copier and make copies of each page. The final result will look somewhat like a car magazine. You don't have to own all the cars in your catalog. Just know that you can get these types of vehicles if you receive an order.

The first page of your catalog should be a letter of introduction, stating who you are and what you do. The letter should be in English and the language of the country you are visiting. Contact a college or language school for assistance with preparing the translation. Don't worry if you can't get it done before leaving home. Have it translated and typed at your hotel when you arrive.

You should also have business cards with your address, telephone and fax numbers. On the back of your card, write the name and telephone number of the hotel where you will be staying. Now, buyers can easily contact you at your hotel and place orders while you're in town.

You will also need a purchase order for recording details of each transaction. A two-part carbonless style will be adequate for your first trip. Refer to the Appendix for a sample copy.

After you arrive, ask around to find out where most of the dealers are located. Often zoning regulations require dealers to be located in certain areas of the city. You should try to stay at a hotel near where most dealers are located. On your first trip, this may require changing hotels after the first few days. By doing so, you can save time and make yourself more available to your new buyers.

With your inventory catalog and business cards in hand, go to the dealers and wholesalers throughout the city. Ask for the owner or manager and introduce yourself. Present your letter of introduction and offer your catalog for their review. The catalog will help break the ice and illustrate the types of vehicles you have to offer. Since you know how long it takes to ship the vehicles, tell the buyer you can have any car or truck like the ones pictured, at port, ready for his inspection.

This method of meeting contacts, to me, is one of the best and easiest when starting out. You can see who you are dealing with, the kinds of cars he is selling and immediately answer any questions that may come up. It also builds trust and in the future makes it easier to do transactions over the phone.

Don't expect to get an order from everyone you talk to. Be patient and optimistic and you will eventually get more orders than you can handle. I recommend that you cover each city thoroughly before moving on to the next. You may get lucky and get all the orders you need in one city. If that happens, you can relax and enjoy the free time until your departure day.

Usually, the most difficult trip is your first trip. The language is different, the money is different and the culture is different. Don't let these factors intimidate you. Tell yourself you are an explorer and this is an exciting and profitable time in your life! Each trip will get progressively easier. Orders will come in from past trips and contacts. Now is the time to begin organizing so that you can receive inquiries and orders without having to travel everytime.

One piece of equipment you will need to purchase is a good facsimile machine. Connect your fax to a dedicated phone line so no other calls will interfere with potential orders. Make sure your fax number is printed on your business card. Explain to every buyer you meet, that all they have to do is fax an order to you with an accurate description of what they want to buy. You will locate the car and call them back with the details and price. You can then work out the terms for payment and ship the car without ever leaving your town!

Another technique that works well is place advertising in foreign magazines. Many countries have auto magazines much the same as ours in the United States. If you can't visit the country that interest you, major libraries in the U.S. may carry the magazines. If not, many countries have a branch of their chamber of commerce located in the United States. Get their telephone number from information, their embassy or consulate.

Once you know which magazines offer cars for sale, call or write the magazine and explain that you want to advertise. Design an ad that explains what you do. Explain clearly that you can fill orders for cars and trucks cheaper and faster than anybody else. Include your address, telephone number, and fax number. Some U.S. wholesalers are already doing this in major cities in England, Switzerland and Germany. Plant the seeds, tend the garden and watch your profits grow!

# SHIPPING

# AND

# CUSTOMS

---

Thousands of cars and trucks are exported from ports throughout the United States every day. You can ship from the West coast, Gulf coast, East coast and the Great Lakes.

To arrange shipping, call shipping agents close to you and inquire about their rates. Rates vary with factors such as the size of the vehicle, quantity shipped and whether or not you want to ship in closed containers. Shippers can also arrange insurance, prepare customs documents, off load and store your vehicles at their destination.

Prepare your vehicles for shipping, first by making sure they are mechanically sound. Pay particular attention to brakes, tires and window glass. Customs in some countries will not clear vehicles with worn tires and poor brakes. Trying to get repairs completed in a foreign port can be time consuming and frustrating. Be sure to plan ahead. Next, bring the vehicles to your shippers port or to a designated pick-up area. Complete the paper work and provide the original title or a certified copy of the title and two facsimiles. Be sure you receive and keep a copy of all the shipping documents including your vehicle titles. The shipper will give you the approximate length of time it takes to complete a trip to various destinations. Most estimates are accurate to within two days. See the Appendix for a listing of shippers located throughout the U.S.

When the vehicle arrives, it will be off-loaded and held in customs for inspection, documentation and payment of duties and fees. Unless you intend to drive the vehicle, leave it in customs and avoid paying the fees, at least temporarily. The dealer or individual who buys the car from you can meet you at customs to inspect the vehicle and pay for it. The buyer can also pay the duty and other fees and receive ownership documentation.

One good reason for not immediately claiming the vehicle at customs is as follows. Many countries have a value added tax (V.A.T.) in addition to customs duty. If you claim the vehicle and remove it from customs, you will have to pay both duty and V.A.T., as well as make arrangements to store the vehicle. If a dealer or wholesaler buys your vehicle, he can often avoid payment of at least some of the taxes by declaring that he is shipping to another country or purchasing the car for resale. In this event, you avoid a substantial V.A.T. and therefore an increase in the final price of the car.

# *GETTING*
# *PAID*

Congratulations! You've made contacts, arranged a transaction, shipped the vehicle and now you would like to get paid. Here are some typical arrangements.

## CASH IN ADVANCE

The safest and best method would be cash in advance. The benefits are numerous and self-evident. Unfortunately, most buyers will not be willing to pay you in advance for vehicles they have not seen, especially if this is their first transaction with you.

## DEPOSIT WITH ORDER

You and the buyer negotiate a reasonable deposit, for example 10%, payable to you with the order. The balance of the contract will then be paid when the vehicle arrives and is inspected. Again, most buyers will be reluctant to hand over money if this is your first transaction. To resolve this problem and to make you and the buyer more comfortable, make an agreement that a third party , such as a bank or attorney, will hold the deposit in escrow until certain conditions are met.

## CASH ON DELIVERY

You take the order, ship the vehicle and receive full payment when the vehicle arrives at port and is inspected by the buyer. Your degree of exposure is greatest in this case because the buyer could change his mind at any time or reject the vehicle once it arrives and is inspected.

Although, your exposure will be greatest with this method it could, at least in the beginning, be your only realistic alternative. To gain some degree of protection, ask your buyer to contact you immediately if there is any change in his intentions. Your risk is also greatly reduced if you deliver the vehicle in exactly the same condition as promised. Lastly, if the transaction does go sour, you can always sell the vehicle to another buyer.

## PERSONAL OR COMPANY CHECKS

Do not accept either unless the check is cashed **before** the vehicle and documents are released. The last thing you want to do is spend time and money trying to deal with the legal system of an unfamiliar country.

## PAYMENT ON A COLLECTION BASIS

The following methods of payment involve both your bank and the bank of your buyer. It is one of the most common methods of buying and selling in foreign markets.

Using this method you receive a draft from the buyer. You then submit the draft and copies of other documents such as the title, purchase order, bill of lading, etc., to your bank. Your bank then forwards these documents to your buyers bank.

A draft as you recall, is a negotiable banking instrument much like a check. When certain conditions are met, the draft can be presented for payment. In order for a draft to be negotiable it must be:

- signed by the drawer (your buyer)
- payable to you or your assigns
- payable for a certain sum of money
- payable on demand or a specific amount of time.

Following are a few of the most common type of drafts presented for collection.

## SIGHT DRAFTS

A sight draft is a promise to pay once certain documents are presented or other conditions are met. Using a sight draft, you forward copies of all shipping documents, copies of titles, etc., along with the sight draft to the buyers bank overseas. Your bank will instruct the buyers bank to release the documents to the buyer once payment is received. Sight drafts allow you to maintain control of the documents and the vehicle until the buyer presents payment in full. To the advantage of the buyer, he does not have any cash outlay until the documents are presented. He can also inspect the vehicle before he pays.

## CLEAN DRAFT

Using this method, you simply present the draft to the buyers bank for collection. The documentation is sent directly to your buyer or his representative.

## TIME DRAFTS

You and the buyer agree that payment will be made on a specific date or a certain number of days after the draft is presented. This method could allow the buyer to prepare for payment as well as inspect the vehicle when it arrives. Do not allow the vehicle to be released from customs until the draft is paid.

## LETTER OF CREDIT

One of the oldest and most commonly used methods of payment in international trade is a letter of credit. Usually expressed as a formal letter, the bank agrees to undertake on behalf of its' customer, to irrevocably reimburse you, the seller, for documents presented which comply with the terms of the letter of credit.

Using this method, you no longer have to rely solely on the credit or the willingness of the buyer to comply with your agreement. Once the vehicles are shipped and other agreed upon documentation is presented, the bank issuing the letter of credit will pay you.

Call or visit your bank and speak with someone in commercial credit. Explain that you will be exporting to various countries and you would like any help they can offer. If your bank does not deal in international trade, they can usually suggest one that does.

Other methods of payment can be tailored to meet your particular needs. Talk to your customers and then have your banker and attorney format the agreement.

# FINAL
# THOUGHTS

---

The best way to learn anything is to simply get involved and start doing it. Start small, gain confidence and expand from there. All of us make mistakes and you will probably have your share. Don't allow anyone or anything to discourage you. Keep trying and persisting and you will succeed beyond your wildest expectations.

# APPENDIX

## Trade magazines and trade organizations

**Automotive News:** Telephone 313-446-6000
1400 Woodbrige Avenue, Detroit, MI. 48207-3187
**Automotive Market Report:** Telephone 412-281-2338
P.O.Box 1317, Pittsburgh, PA. 15230
**National Independent Automobile Dealers Association(NIADA):** Telephone 817-640-3838
2521 Brown Blvd., Arlington, Texas 76006-5203

### Dealer Auto Auctions

Spirit Dance Publishing offers a book listing nearly 300 auctions throughout the United States, Canada and Europe. For more information or to order **The Auction Book**, contact: Success Unlimited • P.O. Box 2006 • Santa Fe, NM • 87504, or call toll-free, 1-800-223-5333.

### Partial Listing Of Dealer Auctions
### Southeast

**Florida:** Florida Auto Auction Telephone: 407-656-6200

West Palm Beach Auction  Tele. 407-790-1200
**Georgia:** Atlanta Auto Auction,    Tele. 404-762-9211
**Alabama:** Auto Dealers Exchange    Tele. 205-699-1010
**South Carolina:** Carolina Auction, Tele. 803-231-7000
**North Carolina:** Statesville Auction Tele. 704-876-1111

### Northeast

**New York:**   Tri-state Auto Auction  Tele. 315-699-9620
State Line Auto Auction Tele. 607-565-8151
Northway Exchange Inc. Tele. 518-371-7500
**New Jersey:** Skyline Auto Auction    Tele. 201-227-0100
Auto Dealers Exchange    Tele. 609-298-3400
**Massachusetts:** Concord Auto Auction Tele. 508-263-8300
American Auto Auction Tele. 508-823-6600
**Pennsylvania:** Manheim Auto Auction  Tele. 717-665-3571
Butler Auto Auction    Tele. 412-452-5555
**Virginia:** Harrisonburg Auto Auction Tele. 703-434-5991
**Kentucky:** Bowling Green Auction    Tele. 502-781-2422

### North

**Michigan:** Flint Auto Auction     Tele. 313-736-2700
Grand Rapids Auto Auction Tele. 616-669-1050
Kalamazoo Auto Auction    Tele. 616-679-5021
**Ohio:**  Northfield Auto Auction     Tele. 216-467-8280

Columbus Fair Auto Auction   Tele. 614-497-2000

Montpelier Auto Auction      Tele. 419-485-3101

**Illinois:** Greater Chicago Auction   Tele. 312-597-3600

Quad-City Auto Auction   Tele. 309-796-1969

Morton Auto Auction      Tele. 309-263-7467

**North Dakota:** Tri-State Auction   Tele. 701-282-8203

**Indiana:** Indianapolis Auto Auction Tele. 317-298-9700

**Wisconsin:** Metro Milwaukee Auction  Tele. 800-662-2947

### Mid-West

**Texas:** Dallas Auto Auction         Tele. 214-264-2344

San Antonio Auto Auction   Tele. 512-661-4200

Gulf States Auto Auction   Tele. 214-288-7585

**Oklahoma:** Dealers Auto Auction     Tele. 405-947-2886

**Missouri:** St. Louis Auto Auction   Tele. 314-739-1300

166 Auto Auction         Tele. 417-882-1666

**Colorado:** Colorado Auto Auction    Tele. 303-287-8077

### West

**Arizona:** Southwest Auto Auction    Tele. 602-894-2211

Arizona Auto Auction     Tele. 602-894-2400

**New Mexico:** Albuquerque Auction    Tele. 505-242-9191

**Nevada:** Nevada Auto Auction        Tele. 702-361-1000

**California:** South. Calif. Auction   Tele. 714-822-2261

L.A. Dealers Auction     Tele. 818-573-8001

Bay Cities Auto Auction Tele. 415-786-4500

Sacramento Auction    Tele. 916-991-5555

Calif. Dealers Exchange Tele. 714-996-2400

**Northwest**

**Oregon:** Portland Auto Auction    Tele. 503-286-3000

**Utah:** Brasher's Auto Auction    Tele. 801-322-1234

**Washington:** Puget Sound Auction    Tele. 206-735-1600

**Canada**

**Toronto:** Toronto Auto Auction    Tele. 416-275-3000

**Oshawa:** Oshawa Dealers Exchange    Tele. 416-576-6633


**Shipping agents shipping to most international ports. Additional listings can be found in the telephone directory of major cities.**

**Affordable Shipping, Inc.:** Telephone 1-800-486-1091

100 Dunbar Avenue, Oldsmar, Florida 34677

**Car Shipping International:** Telephone 305-577-0041

760 Northwest 72nd. Street, Miami, Florida 33150

**Kaiser Shipping:** Telephone 305-592-1339

3409 NW 72nd. Avenue, Unit B, Miami, Florida 33122

**Tampa International Forwarding:** Tele. 813-877-1687

4611 N. Hale Avenue, Tampa, Florida 33614

**Richard Boas & Co.:** Telephone 212-480-9038
29 Broadway Suite 1608, New York, N.Y. 10006
**I.C.E. Inc.:** Telephone 713-987-7501
15311 Vantage Parkway West, Houston, Texas 77032
**Gladish Export Services:** Telephone 213-435-8501
215 Long Beach Blvd. Long Beach, CA. 90802
**Direct Express Inc.:** Telephone 213-608-2100
20505 Annalee Avenue, Carson, CA. 90746
**DOA Enterprises:** Telephone 213-680-1600
Los Angeles, California
Specializing in service to Japan.
**Richard Boas & Co.:** Telephone 213-495-7233
200 Oceangate,Ste. 500, Long Beach, CA. 90802

**U.S. Agencies That Encourage Foreign Trade**
**National Export Traffic League**
234 Fifth Avenue Rm. 301
New York, N.Y. 10001-7607  Tele. 212-697-5895
**Opportunity International**
360 W. Butterfield Road
Elmhurst, Illinois 60126-5025  Tele. 708-279-9300

**Overseas Private Investment Corp.**
1615 M Street NW
Washington, D.C. 20527-0001   Tele. 202-457-7010

**U.S. Dept of Commerce Export Administration**
14th. Street & Constitution Ave. NW Room 3886C
Washington, D.C. 20230-0001   Tele. 202-377-5491

**U.S. Dept. of Commerce International Trade Adm.**
14th. Street & Constitution Ave. NW Room 3850
Washington, D.C. 20230-0001   Tele. 202-377-2867

**U.S. Trade & Developement Program**
1621 N. Kent Street Room 309
Rosslyn, VA 22209-2101    Tele. 703-875-4357

**Foreign Embassies In The United States.**
**Austria:** Telephone 202-843-4474
2343 Massachusetts Ave. NW
Washington, D.C. 20008-2803

**Bahrain:** Telephone 202-342-0741
3502 International Drive NW
Washington, D.C. 20008-3035

**Bulgaria:** Telephone 202-387-7969

1621 22nd. Street NW

Washington, D.C. 20008-1921

**Canada:** Telephone 202-682-1740

501 Pennsylvania Ave. NW

Washington, D.C. 20001-2114

**Czechoslovak Republic:** Telephone 202-363-6315

3900 Linnean Avenue NW

Washington, D.C. 20008-3803

**Denmark:** Telephone 202-234-4300

3200 White Haven Street NW

Washington, D.C. 20008-0000

**Egypt:** Telephone 202-232-5400

2310 Decatur Place NW

Washington, D.C. 20008-4010

**Finland:** Telephone 202-363-2430

3216 New Mexico Avenue NW

Washington, D.C. 20016-2745

**Germany:** Telephone 202-298-4000

4645 Reservoir Road NW

Washington, D.C. 20007-1918

**Great Britain:** Telephone 202-462-1340

3100 Massachusetts Ave. NW

Washington, D.C. 20008-3605

**Hungary:** Telephone 202-362-6730

3910 Shoemaker Street NW

Washington, D.C. 20008-3811

**Iceland:** Telephone 202-265-6653

2022 Connecticut Avenue NW

Washington, D.C. 20008-6131

**Israel:** Telephone 202-364-5500

3514 International Drive NW

Washington, D.C. 20008-3035

**Kuwait:** Telephone 202-966-0702

2940 Tilden Street NW

Washington, D.C. 20008-1193

**Luxembourg:** Telephone 202-265-4171

2200 Massachusetts Ave. NW

Washington, D.C. 20008-2877

**Morocco:** Telephone 202-462-7979

1601 21st. Street NW

Washington, D.C. 20009-1002

**Netherlands:** Telephone 202-244-5304

4200 Linnean Avenue NW

Washington, D.C. 20008-3809

**Poland:** Telephone 202-234-3800

2640 16th. Street NW

Washington, D.C. 20009-4202

**Romania:** Telephone 202-232-4747

1607 23rd. Street NW

Washington, D.C. 20008-2809

**Saudi Arabia:** Telephone 202-342-3800

601 New Hampshire Avenue NW

Washington, D.C. 20037-2498

**Switzerland:** Telephone 202-745-7900

2900 Cathedral Avenue NW

Washington, D.C. 20008-3499

**United Arab Emirates** Telephone 202-338-6500

600 New Hampshire Avenue NW Suite 740

Washington, D.C. 20037-2488

**Yugoslavia:** Telephone 202-462-6566

2410 California Street NW

Washington, D.C. 20008-1614

# *APPENDIX*

Following are examples of typical forms used in the automobile business. The size of the forms have been reduced to accommodate the size of the pages in this book. Most of these forms can be found at office supply stores. If not, your local printer can print them for you.

# Illustration of an odometer statement.

## ODOMETER DISCLOSURE STATEMENT

Federal law (and State law, if applicable) requires that you state the mileage upon transfer of ownership. Failure to complete or providing a false statement may result in fines and/or imprisonment.

I,_____, state that the odometer
(transferor's name — PRINT)
(of the vehicle described below) now reads_____(no tenths) miles and to the best of my knowledge that it reflects the actual mileage of the vehicle described below, unless one of the following statements is checked.

☐ (1)  I hereby certify that to the best of my knowledge the odometer reading reflects the amount of mileage in excess of its mechanical limits.

☐ (2)  I hereby certify that the odometer reading is NOT the actual mileage. WARNING — ODOMETER DISCREPANCY.

| MAKE | BODY TYPE | | MODEL | |
|---|---|---|---|---|
| VEHICLE ID-NUMBER | | | STOCK NUMBER | |
| COLOR | | TRIM | | YEAR |

TRANSFEROR'S PRINTED NAME (SELLER)

TRANSFEROR'S STREET ADDRESS

| CITY | STATE | ZIP CODE |
|---|---|---|

DATE OF STATEMENT          TRANSFEROR'S SIGNATURE (SELLER)

_____  X_____

X_____
PRINTED NAME OF PERSON SIGNING

TRANSFEREE'S PRINTED NAME (BUYER)

STREET ADDRESS

| CITY | STATE | ZIP CODE |
|---|---|---|

RECEIPT OF COPY ACKNOWLEDGED

X_____
TRANSFEREE'S SIGNATURE — BUYER                    DATE

X_____
PRINTED NAME OF PERSON SIGNING                    DATE

102-3

# Sight Draft

ODOMETER STATEMENT MUST ACCOMPANY
TITLE OR DRAFT WILL BE RETURNED

**SIGHT DRAFT**

FLORIDA NATIONAL BANK

**THE AUTO BROKER**

Investment — Wholesale — Retail

Date: _____, 19 ___

Stock No.: _____

PAY TO THE
ORDER OF _____

$ _____

_____ DOLLARS

Supporting Documents: Title enclosed.

Year: _____     Color: _____     Odometer: _____     ID No.: _____

Make & Model: _____

Cyls.: _____

I certify odometer reading at time of sale to be: _____ Miles

Signed _____

Date _____

- ☐ Automatic
- ☐ Power Steering
- ☐ Power Brakes
- ☐ Factory Air Conditioning
- ☐ Other Air Conditioning
- ☐ Radio

- ☐ Vinyl Top
- ☐ Heater
- ☐ White Wall Tires
- ☐ Mag Wheels
- ☐ Power Seats
- ☐ Power Windows

By _____

# Bill Of Sale

## AUTOMOBILE BILL OF SALE

**KNOW ALL MEN BY THESE PRESENTS:**

That in consideration of............................................................Dollars ($ ..............)

to me in hand paid by ...................................................the receipt of which is hereby acknowledged,

I. ..............................................by these presents do bargain, sell and convey to the said

Buyer the following automobile, as is, Make........................................Model...............................

Engine No..........................Serial No...........................License No...........................

And I, myself, will warrant unto the Buyer that the said automobile is free and clear of any lawful claims and demands of all and every person whatsoever.

I hereby grant to the Buyer the Power of Attorney to sign my name to all papers and to receive all documents, rebates, insurance, etc., in order to complete and secure title and possession of said automobile.

Used automobiles are sold as accepted and are not guaranteed.

And I agree to pay all attorney fees and court costs incurred by any party pursuant to above set forth terms and conditions.

Signed ........................................

Address ........................................

Subscribed and sworn to before me, this .....................day of ........................ 19....

........................................

Notary Public residing at ........................................

# Purchase Order-Wholesale

## Asset Management Company
### "World Wide Automobile Exporters"

### WHOLESALE PURCHASE ORDER

Purchaser _____ Agent _____

Address _____

_____ Phone _____

FAX _____

Enter my order for the vehicle below subject to conditions described.

| QTY | YEAR | MAKE/MODEL | COLOR CHOICE | EQUIPMENT | PRICE |
|-----|------|-----------|--------------|-----------|-------|
| QTY | YEAR | MAKE/MODEL | COLOR CHOICE | EQUIPMENT | PRICE |
| QTY | YEAR | MAKE/MODEL | COLOR CHOICE | EQUIPMENT | PRICE |
| QTY | YEAR | MAKE/MODEL | COLOR CHOICE | EQUIPMENT | PRICE |
| QTY | YEAR | MAKE/MODEL | COLOR CHOICE | EQUIPMENT | PRICE |

TOTAL

REC. _____ DEPOSIT

BALANCE TO BE PAID UPON DELIVERY

I agree to deliver the above car(s) with all extras intact and in exactly the same condition as when purchase price was agreed upon.

Shipping Date _____ 19 _____

Completion Date _____ 19 _____

Port of Delivery _____

Other Comments _____

_____

_____

Date _____ 19 __

_____        _____
ASSET MANAGEMENT CO.                                     SIGNED (BUYER)

_____
ADDRESS

_____
PHONE                          FAX

# GLOSSARY

**Agent:** An individual who acts as a representative of a licensed dealer or wholesaler.

**Arbitration:** The process of involving an impartial third party to determine if a mechanical problem exist and then determining the remedy.

**Black book:** A wholesale price guide used to determine the value of cars and trucks.

**Block:** The area where a vehicle is displayed while bidding takes place.

**Detail:** The thorough cleaning of a vehicle to prepare it for sale.

**Draft:** A negotiable banking instrument, payable when certain conditions are fulfilled.

**Eye-appeal:** The general attractiveness of a vehicle based on appearance and popularity.

**Float-time:** The amount of time between when you receive a vehicle and when you actually pay for it.

**Floor plan:** a credit line, usually extended by a bank, for the purpose of purchasing vehicles by a licensed dealer.

**Front line ready:** The vehicle is both mechanically and cosmetically ready to sell, for example, on the front row for maximum exposure.

**Gray market:** Vehicles manufactured in foreign countries not intended for export to The United States.

**No title:** The vehicle title is not present at the time of sale. The title must be presented later or the sale can be recinded.

**Odometer statement:** A federally required statement verifying the mileage of a vehicle at the time of transfer.

**Power of attorney:** Assigns authority to a designated party to act on behalf of the owner. Also known as a "P.A.".

**Recondition:** The process of preparing a vehicle for resale by detailing and repairing as needed.

**T.M.U.:** An odometer that may reflect incorrect mileage, for example, true miles unknown.

**Unit:** Usually refers to a car or truck for inventory purposes.

**Wholesaler:** An individual or company involved in buying, selling and trading vehicles for resale to dealers and auctions.